Praise for
F the Fairy Tale

"Damona Hoffman is an absolute genius because she makes us realize how to help ourselves not stay stuck and get us on a path to understanding ourselves better. And when we clear the cobwebs of one-sided expectations and societal myths, she helps us get the clarity to move forward in a reality that is beautifully tailored for ourselves. It is a pragmatic and self-respecting place of hope with an actual road map."   —Drew Barrymore

"As a therapist deeply invested in human relationships, I loved reading *F the Fairy Tale*. Hoffman shakes up conventional narratives and invites readers to take control of their love stories with relatable anecdotes, wise insights, and actionable tools to help anyone looking for authentic connection navigate the modern dating landscape."

—Lori Gottlieb, *New York Times*–bestselling author of
Maybe You Should Talk to Someone

"Hoffman's *F the Fairy Tale* is the cold shower *and* cup of warm tea every single needs in today's toxic swipe culture. Not just a no-BS approach to love and dating but also a manual that deserves a spot on every therapist's bookshelf, to maneuver through the process and make smart decisions to set you up for a relationship with legs."

—John Kim (The Angry Therapist),
author of *Single on Purpose*

"If you're serious about finding love, this is the book for you! Drawing on her deep expertise in the world of online dating, and written with her signature wit and candor, Hoffman provides a clear and concise guide to modern dating."

—Logan Ury, author of *How to Not Die Alone* and director of relationship science at Hinge

"In the 1980s when I began broadcasting the radio program *Loveline*, my goal was to help people navigate the complex biological reality of sex and relationships. Today, people confront some of the same persistent myths, as well as many new social, cultural, and interpersonal shifts that have made the romantic landscape far more complex. In a very intelligent and readable book, Damona Hoffman outlines these challenges as well as the pillars for establishing healthy connection. Based on years of her experience working with singles, this book is the compendium of what she has learned through helping people in a real-world context. Entertaining, smart, and fun; the reader will find something here that speaks to them and enhances their dating lives."

—Dr. Drew Pinsky

rewrite the
dating myths and
live your own
love story

F the fairy tale

Damona Hoffman

SEAL PRESS

New York

Seal Press

Hachette Book Group

1290 Avenue of the Americas, New York, NY 10104

www.sealpress.com

@sealpress

Printed in the United States of America

First Edition: January 2024

Published by Seal Press, an imprint of Hachette Book Group, Inc. The Seal Press name and logo is a registered trademark of the Hachette Book Group.

The Hachette Speakers Bureau provides a wide range of authors for speaking events. To find out more, go to hachettespeakersbureau.com or email HachetteSpeakers@hbgusa.com.

Seal books may be purchased in bulk for business, educational, or promotional use. For information, please contact your local bookseller or Hachette Book Group Special Markets Department at special.markets@hbgusa.com.

The publisher is not responsible for websites (or their content) that are not owned by the publisher.

Names and identifying details have been changed.

Print book interior design by Amy Quinn.

Library of Congress Cataloging-in-Publication Data has been applied for.

ISBNs: 9781541602250 (hardcover), 9781541602281 (ebook)

LSC-C

Printing 1, 2023

For Seth, the only Prince Charming I have ever known.
Thanks for co-writing our story.

contents

part III: The Date

part IV: The Future

introduction

I F YOU ASKED ME WHEN I WAS YOUNG WHAT I WANTED TO BE, I definitely wouldn't have said a love coach. I never felt lucky in love and always felt a step behind or slightly out of place. I was never asked to prom (or homecoming, for that matter). My first kiss was during a game of Truth or Dare at age sixteen with some rando named Adam. Or was it Paul? Maybe John. Honestly, I barely remember it, and he probably doesn't either.

Don't get me wrong—I wasn't the nerdy ugly duckling that you might be picturing. I was a cheerleader, I starred in the school plays, I was twice elected to student government, but I was definitely not one of the *It Girls*, the women who naturally know how to attract guys.

When I went to college, I felt like I was the only virgin there. Surveys showed at that time that 65 percent of people had sex in high school (now, twenty years later, that number has dropped to about 55 percent; more on that later). Every time I would go out with my friends, I'd end up holding their coats and purses while my friends chatted it up and gave out their numbers like they were Tic Tacs. I felt worse than invisible. I felt . . . different.

Back then, few people on TV and in magazines looked like me. The standard of beauty in those days didn't account for brown skin; wild, curly hair; and a fuller figure. I didn't see men falling for a woman because of her provocative intellect and snappy sense of humor.

By the time I was an adult, I was a full-on love cynic. I moved to Los Angeles and dove headfirst into my work. I found career success early, getting my first assistant job at CBS in the casting department at the ripe old age of twenty-one. The harder I worked, the more I was recognized and the more it made me want to keep working. My job gave me validation and worth, so it is what I put my effort and attention toward. Chasing boys was a road to heartache, but the harder I loved CBS, the more love it gave me in return.

I'd devised a clear life plan. I would work my ass off for the next ten to fifteen years and then, when I'd sucked up all the love from my career, I would magically meet a man that fit right into my life. I wouldn't leave this coveted (yet exhausting) career as a casting director to have kids, but I told myself that my future husband would somehow make it all work.

My boss at CBS was light-years ahead of me. She had followed the same path twenty years earlier and ended up in a loveless marriage supporting two kids and a husband on her executive salary while he shuffled from gig to gig. She filed for divorce and made dating her top priority. This new thing called online dating was all the rage for forty-something divorcées and dudes in their moms' basements, or so I thought.

It was impressive, nonetheless, that she would line up two or three dates after work before she had to pick up her kids from her ex's house. At one point, she was even in a relationship with the CEO of a global ice cream chain. I couldn't believe he was on the dating site. His mom must've had a very nice basement.

Meanwhile, I would often stay out until midnight with some actor/poet/musician who seemed more interested in what I could do for them as a casting director than who I was as a person.

On one of the many mornings I dragged my hungover bones into the office, my boss stared into my bloodshot eyes, poorly disguised after a night of brokenhearted bawling. "I don't like these guys you're going out with," she said, concerned. "You should try online dating." I literally LOLed. Online dating was not for successful women in their twenties. I met tons of men. I went out all the time. I had excuse after excuse at the ready.

Yet as I stared at my Dickensian Ghost of Dating Future, it began to make sense. Those days, the barrier to entry for online dating was high. Your cell phone did not have a data plan, let alone a camera that could take usable profile photos. I would have to scan a printed photo into a computer. Of course I didn't have a scanner at home, so I'd have to go to Kinko's (in the pre-FedEx era).

Swallowing my pride, I asked the cute guy behind the counter to help me scan some solo shots of me onto a disk. No, not a thumb drive, a physical disk. Mortified and certain that he assumed I'd crawled out of my mom's basement for this task, I took the disk back to my home desktop computer, dialed up onto the internet, and transferred the files to my dating site. It was work, but it was worth it. By the next week, I was rolling in messages and potential dates.

Turns out, my boss and I had a hidden superpower useful for online dating. As casting directors, we looked at pictures of people all day. We skimmed through photo after photo, tossing most but always looking for that diamond in the rough who would make us stop and pay attention, that intriguing shot that made us feel like we knew the actor just from the curious expression on their face.

Our years of experience in audition rooms meant not only were we good at picking the cream of the crop but also we understood what it took to be chosen. We knew just how to present ourselves to get picked out of a crowd, how to distill our essence into a single look, how to tell our personal stories through our photos. Then, when we went on dates, we understood that our job was to be charming, to listen well, and to leave them wanting more. A headshot was to a dating profile photo what an audition was to a first date. We were online dating wonder women and we were casting ourselves into the love stories of our lives.

But this wasn't just a game to me. Sure, I was good at getting dates, but I never lost sight of the ultimate goal: to find my partner and to truly be loved. I discovered that as I leaned into the things that made me unique, I attracted better matches for myself. All of those quirks, crazy stories, and embarrassing experiences that I thought made me different (see: undatable) when I was younger were actually the things that people were interested in learning more about. As I unpeeled the layers and showed my authentic self, I attracted authentic love.

It took two years of fine-tuning my online dating strategy for me to meet the leading man I was looking for. He went by the name of Mr. Pandemonium, which I now find ironic considering he's the most grounded, methodical person I've ever met—Seth, the quintessential Virgo. By the third date, I knew he was different, too, but different in the best way.

Seth also had struggled with finding love and felt like he'd squandered his valuable college years. He'd figured that, statistically speaking, college was his best chance at finding his wife. At school, he was surrounded by more smart, single women than he'd ever be again in his entire life. The odds were in his favor to find his match before graduation. But his mission was unsuccessful, and instead he moved to Los Angeles to pursue a career in screenwriting. If he made it, this could be an alternative path to attracting an incredible wife. Yet if he failed, he'd be relegated to the classification of most undatable men in Hollywood: unemployed screenwriter. Lucky for him, our love story took off and, later, so did his writing career.

Soon after meeting Seth, I became an accidental expert in online dating. Friends and relatives started asking for my secrets. I gave them feedback on their photos, helped them rewrite their bios, and counseled them after dates. One amazed friend would tell another, and before long, I was the profile whisperer. I didn't intend to be an online dating coach. I was still planning to become Vice President of Programming. Yet the longer I kept up my side hustle, the stronger the pull became to help more people.

In 2010, I launched my original dating blog, Dear Mrs D, and I also birthed something else into the world—our first child. And I got that VP title. Then I walked away from it to do what I know I was meant to do, help people find love.

Since that time, I've helped thousands of daters navigate the new normal in dating. I worked with Jdate and Match.com when they were still dating "sites," and I became the official Dating Coach of the OkCupid dating app in 2021.

My prior television experience prepared me well for giving dating and relationship advice on air. I've hosted two series for A&E Networks: *#BlackLove* and *A Question of Love*, then I became the Resident Love Expert for *The Drew Barrymore Show*. Now *Dates & Mates*, the podcast that began as a labor of love in 2012, has hit many top ten lists, was named Best Black Podcast of the Year by the Black Podcasting Awards in 2022, and, as of the writing of this book, is still growing. I started matchmaking and writing for the long-running *Washington Post* column Date Lab. Then, the *LA Times* asked me to write an advice column answering relationship questions. I guess it's time to admit that I am no longer a love cynic. I'm a love guide. I lead people to understand their true self so they can attract their true love. It's an unbelievably fulfilling and satisfying career. But as with any worthwhile venture, it has its share of challenges.

WHAT'S GOING WRONG?

If you're reading this book, I don't have to tell you that something is terribly wrong with dating right now. Though we have more options than ever before, dating dissatisfaction is at an all-time high.

It's become cliché to hate on dating. Entire TikTok accounts are devoted to roasting poorly crafted dating profiles. The topic of brunch conversation for most singles today is how awful their dates were that week. At the most horrifying extreme, disillusioned men who we now call incels (short for involuntary celibates) have hurt or killed people because they can't find women to have sex with them.

Contrary to popular opinion, this is not a failing of dating apps. This is not the downfall of romance as we know it. This is a result of the changing way we interact in the world today, a way of communicating that can strip away our humanity and isolate us. The more separate we feel from others, the more we push away the very thing we crave most: love. Then we're left scanning social media for attractive photos that only make us judge ourselves or look down on others.

There are more single adults living in the United States than ever before in history. In 2021, the US Census reported 126.9 million unmarried people over the age of eighteen. That means nearly half of the American adult population is carrying out their lives under a new set of societal norms.

Singles are having less sex than ever before. Sociologists refer to the current period as the sex recession. According to a 2018 article in *The Atlantic*, people in their early twenties now are two and a half times as likely to be abstinent as Gen Xers were at that age; 15 percent report having had no sex since they reached adulthood (see, I was ahead of the curve there).

In the United States, about 60 percent of adults under age thirty-five now live without a spouse or a partner. In 1960, a mere 13 percent of adults lived alone. On the other end of the spectrum, there were fifteen million single mother–headed households in the United States in 2019. This is three times the number in 1960. People are choosing to be alone, delaying marriage, and ending relationships at significantly higher rates than just a few decades ago.

Those in relationships seem to be less in love than ever before. Divorce rates have stopped rising and are holding steady at around 45 percent, but married couples are less intimate and report lower levels of relationship satisfaction than ever before.

Why is everyone so unhappy in love? The relationship ideals we grew up with and societal norms changed faster than our biological relationship conditioning and we are struggling to keep up. This constant inner dissonance between what we want and what we think we need is creating rampant dissatisfaction among couples and singles alike. We have come to believe that we are born knowing how to attract a partner, how to connect, and how to maintain a partnership over time—but this is a false narrative. We look to our collective past for guidance, only to find that the old norms no longer apply or, worse yet, they've misled us in this new normal. It's crucial that we learn how to adapt our beliefs and lean on the true cornerstones that have remained constant in relationships so we can keep love alive at a time when many are ready to give up on it.

FREE YOUR MIND . . . AND THE REST WILL FOLLOW

We don't just wake up one day hating dating or despising our partner. We become disappointed and disillusioned through unmet expectations that seem to build from one frustrating experience to the next. This is driven by our confirmation bias, which occurs when our brain looks for patterns and connections. Our mind is conditioned to tell us stories and identify commonalities that confirm our original hypotheses.

Have you ever had what you would classify as a bad day? Perhaps you woke up late, and then in your rush to get to work, you spilled coffee on your shirt. Those two actions were probably only correlated with you being in a rush and not being careful, but you start to line up the bad day story in your mind. Then, you get to work and your boss calls an unexpected meeting, another bad moment. From that point on, everything that happens that fits into the bad day category is flagged. Anything that is in the good or neutral day category is overlooked. No matter how many compliments or thank-yous or hugs from friends you receive, your confirmation bias has trained your brain to see only the information that confirms your bad day theory.

Similarly, I get email after DM after voicemail from listeners and clients telling me that no one on their dating app ever messages them, but when I look under the hood, I find that they have tons of messages, only they've mentally (and sometimes physically) filtered out dozens of matches because they don't align with the prevailing narrative of "no messages."

A couple duds or an awkward moment can make you believe you are doomed in the dating department and can train your brain to go into each relationship with a defensive mindset.

Just as our brains can default to looking for the negative data points, we can retrain our brains to perceive our experiences differently. We can change our perspective by asking the right questions and having a mind that is curious about the way we think.

Many people write in to my podcast seeking prescriptive advice for a specific dating or relationship question. They want a formula that will help them know what to do in a complex situation. I have distilled my dating system into an easy step-by-step program, but I'll be the first to admit that results may vary. You can learn math through a textbook because math is absolute—a series of steps, when applied correctly, gives you the correct answer.

Yet with relationships, we learn . . . well, relationally. I can give someone my dating playbook, but shifts will happen in their life only when it's put into practice. With each piece of new information we receive, we have to be able to adapt and reapply ourselves in a different way.

People often ask me if they should postpone dating until they've had therapy, lost those last ten pounds, or gotten their promotion. Why wait? You won't be a finished human by then. There will always be new challenges to address and new things to learn about yourself, so why not start now where you are? Plus, don't you want someone to love the real version of you and not some idealized, perfect facade that you can't keep up indefinitely?

If you're unhappy in your relationship but afraid to do anything about it, the problems will not just work themselves out. Why wait until the conflicts are so painful that you have no choice but to face them head-on? Experience is your greatest teacher if you are willing to sit in the classroom of life and learn. We look at healthy couples and assume they must not have any problems, but the truth is, usually they've hit many speed bumps and used them as opportunities to improve their relationship and clarify their communication. Even those steps in the evolution of a relationship are not innately understood and we can and should build skills as our connections deepen and grow.

THE ONLY CONSTANT IN LIFE IS CHANGE

Our experiences are only one part of the puzzle because they are formed from our specific vantage point. Perspective is everything. This book is an invitation for you to flip your point of view and see what you can learn about yourself when you look at your life and choices through another lens and through the eyes of your current or future partner.

All of our prior experiences, from family of origin to past relationships, organize our brains to seek out certain qualities and be repelled by others. At one point in our animal brains, this was a helpful strategy. Early man had to learn on their feet. It was literally a matter of life or death. If you trusted someone of a different tribe and they took your food, shelter, or sense of safety, you and those you loved were toast. You had to learn from your mistakes and adapt quickly.

These learnings were adapted into stories. Initially, the stories were passed down through oral tradition. Later, they were written down and memorialized for future generations to teach us how to make the right decisions that would keep us safe. This contributes to our love of storytelling because, for many centuries, that's how we learned. Our brains are wired to look for patterns and to tell ourselves stories because that is what our ancestors had to do to get by.

Yet in the last 150 years, societal developments have completely changed the way we relate to one another, and we're struggling to synthesize this new information quickly and apply it to our rapidly changing world. Three factors that you might not associate with love have changed our dating and relationship wants and needs the most: travel, technology, and feminism.

TRAVEL

Think about travel over the last century. Early automobiles were expensive and inaccessible to many. If you lived in a city where you could take public transportation, you'd have to devote your day to getting from here to there. Therefore, most of the people you interacted with were from your immediate neighborhood. TV and cell phones weren't a twinkle in engineers' eyes. Your only understanding of things outside your day-to-day world came from stories you read or were told.

Most of the people in your life led relatively similar lives to yours. You probably frequented the same places your friends and family went. You didn't even know numerous places existed and, because of language, distance, and financial barriers, they remained shut off to you.

Enter the proliferation of the automobile and the advent of commercial air travel. Now you could access far-flung places. As the cost of travel decreased, curiosity about other cultures drove us to explore new places. When we experience something new, our brain forms new neural pathways and we, as a species, get smarter.

As transportation expanded, our ability to meet and spend time with people who were different from us also grew. We not only saw a cultural learning opportunity but also found that diversified genes made for healthier humans.

According to analysis by a University of Pennsylvania sociologist, Philadelphia couples who filed for marriage licenses in 1932 lived within five blocks of their betrothed. However, as we ventured farther from home, our dating pool grew rapidly.

TECHNOLOGY

The next big development to change our relational brains was the internet. Technology has advanced so rapidly in the last thirty years that our brains are scrambling to adapt to the continual drip of dopamine reward notifications. Every time you get an email, a like, a notification on an app, your brain sends a signal that says, "Yay, I like that, give me more." But like any addiction, the more we get, the more we crave, and ultimately when we don't get what our brain desires, we hit a depressive slump.

This is the primary reason why dating today feels harder. We have more highs and lows. We are constantly getting our hopes up and constantly having them dashed before our eyes, sometimes in a matter of a few minutes and sometimes without ever actually talking to our rejector face-to-face.

Technology has also given way to new modes of communication. Email and texting have tipped us toward one-way, asynchronous communication. The average modern brain is conditioned to take in more than just words on a page to understand intent and emotional content. Body language, inflection, and other nonverbal cues are missing in text-based communication, and yet our drive for efficiency has made texting the preferred method of conversation, especially in awkward new relationships.

Without the ability to respond in real time or to ask clarifying questions, there's an opportunity for miscommunication as we read between the lines. Convenient and efficient, yes. Clear and emotional, no. Originally, I told my clients that texting was for information and not conversation, but about a decade ago I realized that many of the questions I received related to how to interpret or respond to a text, so I began to see texting as a new skill that needed to be developed.

Around that time, I also began to see the opportunity in video communication. After leading a number of clients through long-distance courtships that would have scarcely been possible before video chat, I embraced video dates as a viable way to get to know someone. When the pandemic hit, everyone soon knew my secret, but not everyone had the playbook for how to do it mindfully, and it left many daters feeling overexposed and even more emotionally depleted than before. Video dating is here to stay, and like texting before it, video will forever change the courtship process—I believe for the better.

FEMINISM

Beyond just the availability of more mate options, feminism and advancements for women are also driving a complete shift in the function of relationships and marriage. Women are no longer just an extension of their parents' property, goods to be bartered to sustain the livelihood of the family. As women became able to support themselves financially, the role of marriage shifted toward one of companionship and love.

The average age of marriage is on a steady upward trend. According to US Census data, the median age of first marriage in 1950 was 22.9 years for men and 20.3 for women. Those numbers were relatively stable for the next twenty-five years and started inching up around 1975. Every ten years or so since, the median age of first marriage has gone up in small increments, until recently when it jumped dramatically. In 2021, the average first marriage age reached 30.4 for men and 28.6 for women.

The timing is curious because 1975 is also the year when women first had the ability to take out loans to buy property without having a man cosign for them. Women becoming independent and able to support themselves is directly correlated to women choosing to marry not out of necessity but out of a desire to partner up. As many women prioritized attaining their own financial security over finding a partner, they committed their twenties to building a career and put finding romantic commitment on the back burner.

This was all happening a few years after birth control for unmarried individuals was legalized by the Supreme Court in 1972, followed in 1973 by *Roe v. Wade*, which recognized American women's right to choose abortion. These two rulings completely changed the trajectory of relationships. Now a woman could have sex without the consequence of pregnancy or possibly being stuck in a relationship that was never intended to last forever. Women could choose to invest in their career before selecting a partner or having a child. When people have options, they make different life choices.

We have yet to see how the reversal of *Roe v. Wade* will impact dating culture, but based on this data, I bet that the sex recession will become the sex depression in many states.

A DIFFERENT WAY OF DATING AND RELATING

All of these developments in travel, technology, and gender equity happened relatively quickly, leaving us in the awkward middle school years of dating culture. Over the last fifteen years of dating coaching, I've seen a series of common beliefs about love that consistently derail my clients' success. These stories guided the courtship rituals of previous generations and worked quite well during that time of stasis, when the average age of first marriage was stable, when our dating pool was limited to those in our immediate community, and when we had less regard for the societal lines that separated us.

It's time to examine these common courtship beliefs and toss out the elements that no longer fit in today's world. So much has changed in dating and relationships in the last hundred years. Why keep living by the old rules that governed love in a time when computers didn't exist, smartphones were science fiction, and laws were in place to disadvantage many groups that are moving toward equity today?

In this book, I will walk you through the four most common dating myths that govern dating culture today. I'll show you how to question these preconceived notions and I'll offer four new pillars of relationship to reconfigure the way you look for a partner or look at the partner you're with. This is a different way of dating and relating, but we're in a new time, so we all should have access to the revised playbook.

Over the years, I've collected a lot of letters, some through my blog, many on Instagram, others from my *LA Times* column, and most from my podcast, *Dates & Mates*. In this book, you will likely hear your thoughts reflected in some of the questions people have asked me, which I have curated and adapted as teaching tools, or in some of the case studies from my actual clients (with their nonactual names for their privacy).

If you adopt an analytical mind toward these questions and solutions, you will see elements that connect for you and solutions that can be applied to your own love life. No relationship is exactly like the next, and you are the person who holds the keys to unlocking lasting love for yourself.

myths & pillars

DEPENDING ON OUR INPUTS AND BELIEFS, MANY LOVE MYTHS might dominate our quest for true love. We grab onto different narratives that, like a bedtime story or fairy tale, get a slightly new spin every time they're told. However, one constant is that each new relationship always goes through four phases: The Mindset, The Search, The Date, and The Future. But it's not always happily ever after because four major myths complicate these phases: the List Myth, the Rules Myth, the Chemistry Myth, and the Soulmate Myth.

The List Myth shows up when you have a set of desired qualities in a match and are constantly keeping a scorecard for each date. Daters who lead with this myth also generally feel the pressure of a specific timeline for love or marriage that is driven by societal or familial expectations. This myth is most prevalent when we are thinking about dating but have trouble getting started or withdraw from the dating pool because of prior unmet expectations.

The Rules Myth governs those who see dating as a game to be won. They have adopted a tactical mindset about meeting people and sometimes even a robotic approach to dates themselves. The Rules Myth is the one that runs dating culture today. It's why people are so ravenous for books like *The Rules* or *The Game* and are hungry for dating content on Instagram and TikTok. If there's a hack for finding love, we want to know it. This myth crops up in the early stages of the dating process and blocks daters from making fulfilling connections.

The Chemistry Myth is the belief that you need to feel immediate romantic sparks with someone for a long-term relationship to work. As the speed of dating has increased, so has the power of the Chemistry Myth. As we try to shortcut the road to a relationship by steering around red flags, we miss the true markers of relationship success and second-guess our dating and relationship choices.

The Soulmate Myth is the belief that you have one perfect match out there and all you have to do is find them and then you'll be happy. If someone could develop a soulmate finder app, they'd make millions. Of course people would pay to confirm their belief in soulmates, but it's a myth. The pursuit of one perfect match actually prevents us from moving into a fulfilling, committed relationship and staying with someone when the going gets tough.

Each myth is rooted in long-standing traditions and its strength is compounded by our personal experiences. These myths were formed to keep us safe and secure. Yet growth and expansion happen outside the confines of what we already know. There is always risk when you step into the unknown. At a certain point, love is always a leap of faith, but if you're unwilling to take the plunge, you may get yourself stuck inside the web of your own stories.

Which myth is driving your beliefs on love most? Here's a quick pop quiz.

Do you find that it's hard for someone to match up to your criteria? Do people accuse you of being picky? Then you might be stuck on the List Myth.

Do you feel like you're on some kind of cruel hamster wheel of love, always meeting people in a never-ending cycle of dates but never making a real connection? You are likely leaning into the Rules Myth.

Have you met people who appear great but always seem to be missing something that you can't quite put into words? Maybe you're fixating on the Chemistry Myth and you're misinterpreting the signals that your body is sending you.

Do you wish you had a fast-forward button that would enable you to skip the awkward dating phase and just land the love of your life on your doorstep? You probably have fallen for the Soulmate Myth.

Perhaps you connect with more than one of these situations. Perhaps all four! We are focusing on these four myths throughout this book because of how one or another dominates each phase of a relationship, but you might identify an alternative myth as you come to understand the stories that govern your life and the skills that you can build to help you in dating and relationships.

Not to worry, though. For each of the major myths, there is an antidote. When you're ready to leave dating by myth behind, there's a better way to guide your relationship choices: the Four Pillars.

THE FOUR PILLARS

I've been asked hundreds of times by clients in the early stages of dating, "How can I tell if it's going to work out?" I don't have a magic wand, as much as I would love one (though I did make a fantastic Glinda for Halloween in 2015). However, when I was working on the TV show *A Question of Love* with three couples who were all at a major turning point in their relationships, I identified the four elements that illuminated the health and longevity of the relationship. I call them the Four Pillars.

Think of a relationship like a table. If it's built with a solid foundation, it can stand for years. Your family gathers around it and you make memories together. You can build a table with only three legs, but it probably won't last as long as one with four, and what will happen if you put something heavy on it? Can it support the weight? If you build the table with weak, splintered wood, it might look charming for a while, but trust me, it'll get wobbly. Could you serve your holiday dinners on it for generations to come? Your poor child is going to be stuck at the flimsy end with all the heavy dishes constantly sliding in their direction.

You need to start with four strong pillars and build your table on top of them. Of course, you might need to refinish it one day. You might even replace one of the legs down the road, but as long as you and your partner are willing to do the work to set this table up and keep repairing it together, you and this relationship . . . er, table, can last.

As you can imagine, building this table takes some time. You need to source materials, measure them, refine them, and finish them. Then you need to test the table to make sure it's sturdy. When people ask me whether or not their relationship is going to last, I can't give them a quick answer because all of that building hasn't happened yet. They are only looking at a bunch of raw materials and trying to figure out what the finished table will look like years down the road.

We live in an instant-gratification society that pushes us to know the answer to everything immediately. But the exciting thing about relationships is that they are one of the only places left in our lives where we can have discovery, explore our curiosity, and watch something build.

Raising two kids in a world in which technology is integrated into their daily lives, I've seen firsthand how our brains are being rewired. The time between asking a question and discovering the answer has been truncated. Just ask Siri! The quest to explore what is unknown and dance in the open space between curiosity and certainty is disappearing. Currently, machine-learning experts are trying to identify your relationship patterns and reduce your decision-making process to an algorithm so you can truncate this process too. However, as of the writing of this book, such technology does not yet exist. You're going to have to do the work instead, so let's build that table. Let's start with the Four Pillars.

The Four Pillars outlined in this book each correspond to one of the four relationship phases. The first pillar is **GOALS: A shared vision of the future**.

By the time they start dating seriously, most daters have some idea of what they want for their future lives. Do they want kids? What is their long-term career path? Is marriage important to them? These are the kinds of topics that tend to come up early in the dating process and some people even spell them out in their dating profile from day one. Of course, your goals may change down the road, and once you have a partner, you might ask them for support in moving toward a new goal. But in early courtship, goals are front-loaded in the discussion as a first filter.

The second pillar that is vitally important to long-term compatibility is **VALUES: A similar and compatible outlook on the world and the way in which you live your life**. True belief systems begin to emerge as people "stop being polite and start getting real," to quote one of the most famous studies in human behavior, MTV's *The Real World*. After settling into the relationship, you and your partner are no longer on best behavior and that's when you become aware of not only what people say but also who they *are*. Our values tend to be fixed by the time we reach adulthood, so you may be unable to change your partner's mind, but you can better understand their heart and where they're coming from.

This is a core element to healing society's deep emotional wounds. We cannot truly understand another if we are unwilling to engage in the conversation. The best way to build love and empathy for those who are different from us is by actually spending time together and seeing inside their world.

The third pillar is **COMMUNICATION: Clear communication and conflict resolution skills**. Your communication skills will be tested from the start of a relationship. If you can't communicate your relationship goals early on, you will end up having to communicate them later with much more emotional intensity. I recommend you start earlier, when the stakes are lower and you have less invested.

Conflict resolution skills may not come up in the honeymoon phase of dating, but eventually you will hit some sort of a road block and it will test whether you and your partner can resolve conflict together. A relationship without any discord isn't the mark of a successful partnership, just as a relationship with constant drama is not either. You need enough conflict to see whether you and your partner can respectfully disagree and still find common ground.

The fourth pillar that you encounter in a relationship is **TRUST: A feeling of safety and mutual respect**. Interestingly, trust is the foundation of every great long-term relationship, yet it is the pillar that is discovered last because it takes time to build trust with another human. Trust is built as you see that someone's words align with their actions. Trust is built when your person sticks with you through thick and thin. Trust can't be distilled into a BuzzFeed quiz. It has to be shown to you in moments when your relationship is riding on hope and faith that this person will show up for you when you need them.

Now that we know the Four Pillars and the Four Myths, let's see how they correlate so you can better understand which broken beliefs may have driven your past relationships and begin to rewrite them for a brighter future.

SLOW LOVE

As you are rewriting your myths, you will best be able to recognize your patterns and change them by taking your time. The concept of slow love was popularized by Dr. Helen Fisher, a biological anthropologist and senior research fellow at the Kinsey Institute who has spent decades studying how the brain responds to love. I first met Dr. Fisher at Match Group Headquarters in Dallas during a conference when Match.com handpicked the top love coaches in the world to come together and talk about the future of dating.

Slow love is based on scientific research that shows how our brains change so dramatically during the various phases of forming a new relationship that, many times, even the most logical of us can't figure out how we feel. In our quest for a happy ending to our love story, we often rush through the other steps of getting to know a potential partner. The trouble is, once you speed through them, it's hard to go backward, and if you have pressed onward and ignored important details about your compatibility, the pillars of your table are going to be a bit shaky.

To fully understand this, let's unpack some of Dr. Fisher's research. Dr. Fisher and her team examined functional MRI (fMRI) brain scans of people in three romantic situations: those who had just fallen happily in love, those who'd been rejected in love, and those who were in love long term. Dr. Fisher and her team found that different areas of the brain were activated when these people were thinking about love—specifically, the same areas that are activated in addiction.

Another study at the University of Pisa showed that levels of serotonin, a neurotransmitter that regulates feelings of contentment, were similar in people who had recently fallen in love and in people with obsessive-compulsive disorder (OCD). So if you feel like love makes you lose your mind, you're not entirely wrong. Your brain is literally altered and different neurochemicals are released in response to your romantic situation.

Side note: This explains the absolutely bonkers letter I once wrote to my college boyfriend when we broke up. During our summer-long open relationship, he fell for a man who reminded him of me. I'll admit, I never thought we would last in the first place, yet when the breakup happened, I still became hysterical. Not Victorian-style hysterical; actual hysterical: overcome with extreme and illogical emotion. I spewed every thought I had in that letter, but ultimately the outcome of the situation didn't change. I still felt rejected and he still dated men. Thankfully, the evidence of this incident is lost in a landfill somewhere near Lake Michigan.

Perhaps you have a breakup letter you hope the world will never see. Or maybe you are of the generation who wrote their breakup letters publicly on social media and are terrified that these tirades might be dredged up in a Google search one day. Now you have a fine excuse. You were under the influence of powerful brain chemicals and experienced a wild bout of withdrawal when they were suddenly taken away.

This is the emotional roller coaster we ride when we love. We crave the thrill and anticipation, but we want to shortcut the sticky parts, the parts that bring up fear and anxiety. Then, when we are coasting, we start to wonder what happened to the peaks and valleys. We question whether we are still on the ride at all or whether we should hop off and get on a new ride that will give us that zippy feeling again.

Whether we are single or in a relationship, we are just love addicts looking for our next hit of romance. Yet we need to have more than attraction and infatuation for love to last long term. We need to know we have all Four Pillars, that vital foundation for a lasting relationship, before we can build a strong table. You can tell which elements you have only by walking through the gamut of emotions within your relationship.

EMPATHY FIRST

To introduce one of the foundational elements of my philosophy, it's time to bring in a question from a listener.

Dear Damona,
I don't really like dating apps because it feels so impersonal. I've been ghosted several times and it's starting to take a toll on my self-esteem. I'm a nice person and I try to be kind and message someone back if I'm not interested, but rarely do I get the same courtesy when someone isn't into me.

The key to this wild journey ahead lies in an unexpected ally: empathy. The only way we can truly be loved, seen, and cared for is if we embrace the fabric that weaves us all together. One of the biggest downsides of our robust online world is that it often leads to an alternative online identity and way of relating that aren't in alignment with the person we are in real life.

We create a picture-perfect version of ourselves on dating apps or social media. Then we swipe through other human beings with the same speed and lack of attention as we do a store catalog. Operating behind the wall of the online identity you've constructed leads to an inauthentic way of connecting with people in the online world that often bleeds over into how we communicate in person.

This has led to a rise in ghosting—people suddenly disappearing after making a connection. It has also led to more transactional conversations on dating apps and offline. Worst of all, it's given way to a feeling of overall apathy about dating and pursuing the very thing that drives our actions most—the desire to be loved.

This letter writer is ready to scrap dating apps entirely because of the response of a few people who did not get the memo on this. Taking your ball and going home doesn't change the game, it only takes you out of it. It's a loss for you and for the good person who hoped to meet you. So, how can you press on past those disappointments or transform their meaning for you?

The antidote to the pervasive attitude of apathy is simple: It's empathy. When you approach dating with compassion for the other person, regardless of whether you're destined to be together, you can still access a feeling of love and care.

Empathy—being able to understand and share the feelings of another—is rarely applied in dating. Leading with empathy separates us from the transactional nature of meeting someone online and shifts us toward trying to understand those we meet. If we take a step back from being the protagonist in our love story and instead look at the story from other characters' points of view, the read becomes much more interesting.

From the point of view of the narrator, you can see how each person you meet might help your growth or understanding. You can also see that every scene might not be in service of your story but that you might be temporarily playing a role in someone else's story.

The Empathy-First Method adds an important layer to understanding dating today and allows for a deeper level of emotional connection, something we desperately crave but are sorely lacking right now.

You've probably figured out that this book does not offer a list of the "Ten Best Relationship Tips Ever." Did you think that you were reading a how-to book? Sorry to tell you, this is more of a why-how book. Once you truly understand what is driving your decisions in love and *why*, you have the power to shift the path before you and you'll have a far better outcome than if I just told you what to do.

Whether you're in a relationship now or seeking one, this book will unpack all of your "stuff" along with the hand-me-down stuff that you got from your parents, teachers, friends, and grandparents. We will take stock of what you want to keep and what you can let go of. Then we can figure out how to mend the parts of your heart that might be broken and how to heal our collective hearts once and for all.

part I

the mindset

chapter 2

the list myth

ONCE UPON A TIME, THERE WAS A SINGLE WOMAN WHO thought she knew exactly what she wanted in a match. He would be tall, rich, smart, and handsome. She journeyed all across the land looking for her prince, but could not find him. What the woman didn't realize, though, was that everyone else was looking for the same thing and they'd snatched up all the suitors she thought she wanted. Her true love was right there under her nose the whole time, but she was so focused on this list of "high-value traits" that she could not see him.

When frustrated daters come to me for help, my first question is: What are you looking for? Most people believe that they are unique individualists who have developed their own specific list of desirable qualities in a mate, but most people in my practice recite the exact same list to me. Scientists have hypothesized that certain physical traits of attractiveness, such as wider hips in women or a chiseled jawline in men, indicate which matches are evolutionarily preferred. This may have been part of the story before medical advancements and other societal shifts, but I've discovered another possible source of our preferences in the work of Dr. Francis Galton. He is known as the father of eugenics, and his 1869 book *Hereditary Genius* was based on the principle that we could build a superior society if people with more-desirable qualities married and procreated and those who were "feeble-minded," "unattractive," or "of lower status" were sterilized or kept from mating. How did he separate premium people from the inferior ones? With a list—one that measured factors such as height, mental fitness, and income.

We'd like to think that what we want is simply our preference, but when we examine where these beliefs took root, we may discover surprising foundations and ways in which we have unknowingly been influenced by societal expectations. We have been conditioned to value certain qualities but rarely stop to examine whether these factors truly support the life we uniquely are building.

Fast-forward a little more than a century from Dr. Galton's time and the list returned in the form of online dating. Although I love dating apps for their ability to expand our dating pool, they also have the power to limit it when they prompt daters to list superficial qualities about themselves and evaluate matches based on the boxes they've checked as well.

The more popular the apps became and the faster the speed of dating, the more users pushed the apps toward efficiency. Long-form responses got culled, explanations around interests became truncated, and suddenly education, height, career, and physical attractiveness got front-loaded in the search process. Now we've become reliant on both the list and the algorithm to tell us who the best matches are—without questioning whether they *are* the best matches for us.

On the flip side, clients who don't have any list of criteria usually tell me they'll "know it when they see it." They believe this makes them open to anything, but without a framework through which to filter dates, these clients often won't pursue any relationship or they become overwhelmed with options. I believe there's something in between carrying Dr. Galton's list forward and waiting for the answer to land on our doorstep. It begins with changing the criteria you're using to pick your matches.

MUST-HAVES AND DEAL BREAKERS

Making a list confirms the expectation that there is an exhaustive set of criteria that must be met in order for someone to be considered a viable match for a relationship. Having a list of twenty qualities that you are seeking can distance you from having to make any choices about your dating options. If there's always something on the list that your date lacks, you always have an escape hatch that can abort the mission before you get vulnerable or feel rejected yourself.

Daters might think that having a long list expands their possibilities for a good match, but in practice a long list is more limiting because these daters feel like they're settling or they've been cheated if they can't find one person who fulfills everything on their list. This leads them to become discouraged and despondent about dating. Having some criteria is important for filtering purposes, but have too many and it becomes a minefield of reasons *why not* that even the best matches cannot clear.

Begin to break free of the List Myth by getting laser-focused on only the most important personal qualities of a specific match for *you*. The next step is to narrow your list to only three must-haves and one deal breaker to clarify what is essential to you in a relationship. If you can have only three must-haves, you will make your selections mindfully.

Still, there always comes a point when I have to engage in "dating math" with clients. As they build their list, I compute how each selection erodes their dating pool bit by bit. One of the most common must-haves I see from heterosexual women is the "over six feet tall" request, but only about 14.5 percent of men meet this requirement. Want someone with a college degree? That's about 37 percent of the US population today. Make it a master's degree? Now you're down to 14 percent. Layer in location, race, and income and suddenly these limited pools compound to a miniscule dating sample. Then, when we account for age range and subtract everyone who is already partnered, it's no wonder that someone with a list would find dating frustrating. Your micro choices add up to no one being left for you! Narrowing this list down to just three must-have qualities and one deal breaker forces you to identify what matters most to you but keeps your pool deep enough to fish in.

WHAT IS A MUST-HAVE QUALITY?

A must-have usually is something that speaks to who the person is at their core or how they live their life. You might think you need someone who makes a good income, but when we unpack it, you discover that you're actually seeking someone who doesn't drain the resources you worked hard to build. Or perhaps you're seeking a person who saves for the future and isn't frivolous with spending the money they have.

We have to include relationship goals as one of our primary must-haves. When everyone was groomed to be married with children by twenty-five, most daters had similar goals. Now you get to choose whether you want nonmonogamy, parenthood, or even a LAT relationship (meaning living apart together: a committed relationship or even marriage in which the couple lives in separate homes).

As the options have expanded, our need to make choices that support our vision of an ideal life has become more important. This expansion of possibilities is a tremendous opportunity. However, Thomas Edison reportedly said, "Opportunity is missed by most people because it is dressed in overalls and looks like work." As you move toward your specific relationship goals, you might have to eliminate a match who's attractive and fun to be with if they aren't a match on your core needs, and this leaves more work ahead to find your person. Good news, though: you can skip the overalls.

GETTING WHAT YOU WANT

Having clarity about what you want is vital, but you also have to know how to act on it. Here's a question I received from one of my podcast listeners that illustrates this point:

> *Dear Damona,*
> *I am a twenty-six-year-old finance guy living in a small West Coast city. Being my age, I am relatively open to anything. I definitely prefer something more serious, yet I have struggled to find dates. My friends tell me that I would be someone women will want to settle down with and not necessarily date right now. How do I find where I'm going wrong? I want a relationship, but I feel like I'm losing out to men who just want casual sex.*

This letter writer is probably not losing as much to men who want casual sex as he is to *himself* for being open to anything and filling his time with women who don't meet his primary relationship goal. By saying he's someone women would want to settle down with, people may mean that casual dating reads as false on him.

Whatever your perceived dating challenge, instead of competitively comparing yourself to others, try to differentiate yourself. Simply by leading with your dating goal, you'll set yourself apart from the pack and attract someone who prefers that type of relationship. Those who don't align with your relationship goals will find someone else who is "open to anything" or who states a different preference, and the others will be looking for you.

Also, although his friends are probably trying to comfort him about why his prior relationships haven't panned out, their projections actually plant the seed of doubt and make him expect rejection. If you have friends like this, tell them to buzz off about your love life. Dating is not a spectator sport.

DEAL BREAKERS

Deal breakers are often tossed around in casual conversation, but bottom line: they're overused in dating. People tell me that the person snores and that's a deal breaker. Or they chew with their mouth open—deal breaker. Those may be annoyances, but are they qualities that tell you who that person is and how they live their life? Could you find a fix for that particular deal breaker? Even though it's not ideal, could you learn to accept it as one of their quirks?

Even something as divisive as smoking might look (and smell) like a deal breaker on the surface, but it's possible that, as much as you hate it, it might not be an actual deal breaker for you if this person possesses the must-have qualities you are seeking.

Dear Damona,
I matched with someone on a dating app and we started talking. When we went on our first date, he shared that he smokes ciga-rettes (which is usually one of my deal breakers). We really hit it off, but the smoking bothers me. How can you tell if you're being judgmental and a little bit closed-minded to a potential partner who could be a good match?

The "how can you tell if you're being judgmental" part is a common addendum to questions I receive on *Dates & Mates*. Whenever we second-guess ourselves about eliminating a poten-tial match, it's helpful to go back to our core values and try to understand their root meaning. When someone tells me one of their deal breakers, I'm curious to know why. In this case I would ask: Is it that you don't like the smell or taste of cigarettes? Do you know someone else who smoked and associate a particular outcome or experience with them? Do you feel like smoking is in conflict with your lifestyle and values? Then we can get to the root of where this belief comes from and figure out whether it's situational, aspirational, or a true impassable deal breaker.

Yet if you start to judge yourself as closed-minded, you begin to question and compromise your own dating boundaries. Reconnecting to the reason why you established this boundary in the first place can help you understand whether it is truly a value of yours or simply a preference. Preferences can be overlooked if there are enough positive factors to offset them. Boundaries and values can never be overlooked and are a guide for your early interactions with dates.

Perhaps smoking is not on your list of deal breakers, but you can probably relate to a time you questioned whether you were eliminating a potential match unnecessarily. Once we are dealing in actuals instead of hypotheticals, we tend to compromise to make them fit. But the cracks will inevitably show through. If something is a deeply held value of yours, a match can only shapeshift for you so long before returning to their true self. If they've been transparent with you, then next you need to be transparent with yourself.

CASE STUDY: DATING DEATH BY DEAL BREAKER

On certain apps you can exclude anyone who possesses your deal breakers from appearing in your feed. If you never want to see someone who votes blue or goes to church regularly or eats red meat, you never have to. Deal breakers sound amazingly efficient in the filtering process of dating, but use them sparingly.

I was analyzing the dating profile of a client who was concerned that she wasn't seeing any matches. Whenever I hear a declaration like: "There are NO matches for me on this app," I assume the person really means: "No one that I'm attracted to is messaging me . . . yet."

However, there was no hyperbole with this client. When I logged in, my eyes widened in shock. The app said, "Please check back later for more matches." This message sometimes pops up when a dater is new on the app or after they've gone through their allotted matches for the day, but to open a long-standing profile on the app for the first time in months and see absolutely no matches was new to me. I assumed there must be a technical glitch until I audited her search criteria. She had checked only a few qualities in her match preferences, which meant we were already working with a limited pool, and on top of that, she had selected the deal breaker button for five of them. Using the deal breaker feature like this meant that people who might have possessed the other criteria she was looking for but lacked any one of the deal breakers weren't even showing up in her feed. I tested my theory. One by one I lifted her deal breakers and watched her options populate. This was a classic case of dating death by deal breaker.

In my work, I almost always arrive at an uncomfortable conversation with clients about compromising on something they thought was a deal breaker. It's that you have to figure out what your preferences truly mean to you. Is there an emotional need behind them? Are they programmed positively or negatively by past relationships? Are you making assumptions based on your family of origin? Or are your deal breakers really core needs or goals?

The moral of the story is, if you're going to check something as a deal breaker on an app, it better actually be a deal breaker, something that you cannot live with under any circumstance. Moreover, you better just pick *one*. Shifting from chasing a relationship ideal that can never be attained to clarifying your must-haves and deal breakers doesn't happen overnight, but it does happen when you approach dating mindfully and paint a picture for yourself of the life you want to lead. It happens if you truly know your relationship goals.

THE PARADOX OF CHOICE

As they say, there's a lid for every pot, but dating is starting to look a bit more like my Tupperware drawer. I know the lids are in there, I just can't seem to find the one I need at the time. Is it because I have so many sets jammed into the drawer with no organizational strategy? While I ponder that question, I'll share one of the questions I'm asked most on this topic: "Aren't people less likely to want to settle down and choose a partner because they have so many options available right now?" This question is usually inspired by Barry Schwartz's book *The Paradox of Choice*, which proposes that having more choices creates dissatisfaction and overwhelm. According to Dr. Schwartz's research, the crush of options leaves us decision fatigued and unable to be satisfied with the selections we make. In the book, Schwartz identifies two kinds of people in the world. There are Maximizers, who like to look at every option and are on a constant quest to find the perfect one. Even when they make a decision, they tend to reevaluate and question the choice, which leads to tremendous stress and disappointment.

Then there are Satisficers, who clarify their core requirements in any decision, and once those criteria are met, they are satisfied with their choice and put it out of their mind, confident that their selection has been made effectively.

If people can't make a decision about their matches online, why are rates of marriage from dating apps continually increasing? I believe there's a major misunderstanding about the paradox of choice. It's not solely the availability of numerous options that makes people unable to choose. It's the lack of clarity around core selection criteria that leaves us in a state of decision paralysis. Maximizers are not simply so overwhelmed with the number of options that they can't make a choice. They experience unnecessary strife and disappointment with their choices because they are seeking quantity over quality and an unattainable idea of perfection, both by-products of having a fuzzy concept of the qualities they're seeking.

Satisficers are generally more satisfied with their choices because, once they see an option that meets their basic needs, they move confidently forward with their selection. If you date on a quest for a perfect fantasy without knowing the specifics of what you're looking for, you'll always be looking for something that seems just out of reach. Yet if you take the time to date mindfully and with clarity about your search criteria, the field narrows and you can take advantage of the popularity of dating apps that offer lots of options, knowing that you don't have to review them all to make a choice

This is the precise reason why this dating process begins with mindset. Clarify your dating goals and visualize your ideal mate, but base it not on a soulmate idea of perfection but on how you want to feel when you're with this person and what your future will look like together. When you know who you are and what you're looking for, you can sort through your options and make a connection. Those who aren't aligned with you will see you coming a mile away and, yes, they'll run, but those who align with you on the Four Pillars will wonder where you've been hiding all this time. The key is to not get lost in the numbers game and mourn those missed opportunities.

DATING FENG SHUI

Those of you who know me from TV or podcasting probably think of me as having grounded, tactical methods. This is true. What you might not know, however, is that my dating philosophy is also rooted in time-tested spiritual practices, some of which have scientific research backing them up and others for which I can provide only anecdotal evidence.

All this to say, for some, this section is going to get a little woo-woo. But I assure you, everything fits together in the grand dating scheme and I'll get to the more practical aspects of my approach once we have laid this foundation. Finding love is a little yin and a little yang. The clinical term for this in social psychology is *dual processing*, meaning we use both our rational, thinking brain and subtle, intuitive inputs to make decisions, especially when it comes to love. If you are a planner who lives your life by logic, I invite you to surrender to this experience. If you can, you're in for some of the most transformational times of your life.

My friend Inessa Freya left the casting department behind to follow her calling as a feng shui consultant. When she was building her business, she needed client testimonials, so I eagerly volunteered. The ancient Chinese practice was new to me, but the more she explained, the more I embraced it. Most people believe feng shui is a design technique in which you simply move stuff around and your life will change, but it's much more than that.

Feng shui works because it always starts with setting intentions. The style of feng shui Inessa practices doesn't take a one-size-fits-all approach to fixing or "curing" a space. It is a bespoke experience based on a person's individual space and specific desires. She started our sessions with what I hoped to manifest in my life and prescribed different actions to take or elements to bring into my space to make it happen. There was meditation, visualization, and intention setting that had to happen before we could clear a path for the energy to flow in the direction I wanted.

At the time of our initial session, I was also working with a life coach who helped me realize that finding a relationship was of the utmost importance to me. For years, I had hurried myself from activity to activity and barreled through work as a distraction from the thing that I didn't have but deeply desired—partnership.

They say in feng shui, "Where attention goes, energy flows," and all my energy was flowing into my work, friends, and family, leaving nothing for me to pursue a serious relationship, or so I believed. Once my attention was focused on dating, Inessa gave me the activities to help move the energy in the direction I wanted.

After a deep visualization exercise, she gave me a silver container that, in feng shui, is called the "helpful people box" and asked me to fill it with pieces of paper that contained the qualities of the person I hoped to meet. Eagerly, I scribbled note after note about this creative, feminist dream guy. I even imagined that he might be a writer who could work from home so he could be a 50-50 participant in raising our children. As I approached my ninth or tenth adjective that described the man who appeared in my visualization, I looked up at her and blurted out, "This guy doesn't exist."

She stopped me immediately. "Don't judge. It will block the chi." I looked at her quizzically. She explained that *chi* is the energetic flow that brings us harmony. By wishing for something and immediately questioning its existence, I wasn't allowing our work and the chi to take root. I refocused my attention on the task, hoping that she was right, that this unicorn of a human actually did exist and that somehow this activity would send out the Bat-Signal to him.

A few months later, I moved into my own apartment after years of roommate life. I had gotten an amazing promotion at work and felt that unwritten adulting rules required me to live alone at least once in my life. As I sorted through the many papers and knick-knacks on my desk, I found the little silver box. I had nearly forgotten about it and the exercise that Inessa had talked me into a few months earlier, but holding it there in my hands, everything came flooding back.

Since the time I'd set up my "helpful people box," I'd met a great guy, a writer. I didn't know if he was *The One*, but our relationship was so different from those before him that I often wondered if it was too good to be true for me. I cracked open the silver box and peered inside at the collection of paper slips. As I removed the first one, I smiled. It was an adjective that described him to a T. Pulling out the next paper made me chuckle, again a word that was distinctly him. I went through all of the words in that box and every one of them fit this man. They were not peripheral qualities like you sometimes find in drugstore horoscopes that toss around one-size-fits-all language. They were core elements that defined who he was and his life goals.

My head was spinning—I'd thought this person did not exist. Just a few months earlier, I couldn't even picture a guy with these qualities. But now, I was in a relationship with this exact man, who seemed to have been ordered from the great Amazon Prime of the universe. Three and a half years later, I married that man and today it's just as magical as that auspicious feng shui day. He is a self-proclaimed feminist who, like me, believes in an equal partnership. He writes for TV shows like *House* and *The Walking Dead*, yet he makes it a priority to be a hands-on dad who is equally involved in raising our children. I didn't have to know exactly who this person was or where I would find him, but I had to keep a sliver of faith alive that this man did exist and that one day our paths would cross.

Now that I'm married to that man, I can see the difference between the way Inessa helped me visualize my ideal partner and the way I used to date as if I was checking off an inventory list and seeking the same qualities that appealed to everyone else without taking time to really investigate who would be right for me and what my life could look like with the right person. She was absolutely correct, though, I had to set logic aside for a moment and visualize the life I wanted, not just the life that society and experience had told me I could have.

What I needed in a partnership was completely different from what my friends, parents, and relationships I saw in the media required. I had to create space for the life I was building and direct my mind and my actions toward my ideal future, even if it meant dismantling long-held beliefs about gender roles, time-lines, and traditional marriage.

chapter 3

the goals pillar

FINDING ALIGNMENT

Dating by list keeps us in a myopic point of view. When we try to match qualities with boxes we list in our mind (or in some cases on actual paper), it doesn't make way for the matches who fall in between the lines on the list but who might otherwise be great matches for us.

The first thing you need to figure out before you can even begin to consider dating someone is whether or not your life and relationship goals are aligned. Someone could have all the physical characteristics you wish for, but if they are on a different timeline, you'll always feel like you're pushing or pulling them.

An alternative to dating by list is seeking someone whose path is aligned with yours. It's time to replace the List Myth that has been holding us back from finding real connection with the first pillar for a happy, healthy relationship: common goals for the future.

This is so foundational and yet it is often overlooked in the early phase of dating because people are afraid that, if they speak their truth, their date might run away. If you say that you want to have kids, you want to be a stay-at-home parent, you're planning to move out of state, or you'd be happiest in a nonmonogamous relationship, you might scare away a match that has everything on "your list." We have to reframe this. These kinds of life choices should be at the top of your list. The goal of modern dating isn't to be liked by everyone. It is to find the person you are best suited for and build a future with them.

If your deepest desires and vision of the future repel your date, you have to see this as a blessing. You'll save a lot of time, effort, and tears if you learn up front where they stand. Rather than thinking of it as a personal rejection, consider it a rejection of what you are offering in this life you're building right now. It's not that anything is wrong with what you want, it's simply not a fit for them.

REJECTION REFRAME: SPARED OR PREPARED

When you feel rejected, you're either being spared or prepared. You're being spared more heartache or you're being prepared for something greater, something that you wished for but perhaps never dreamed was even possible. It's rarely a rejection of you personally, but, as in the case of many of my clients, it's a rejection of the path you're traveling. They're just headed to a different station on the train of life.

When you have clarity about the life you are building and the relationship you want, it will make those who see a similar future for themselves lean in and it will repel those who don't. You can use this to your advantage instead of tiptoeing around the facts, worried that you'll turn them off if you speak your truth. This approach can also help you manage rejection without internalizing it and taking it personally.

If you notice a pattern of many people pushing you away for the same reasons, then it's worth doing more self-healing and introspection, but in most cases, a rejection says more about them than it does about you. Inessa, my feng shui consultant, told me this affirmation and you can repeat it to yourself in those moments when you question yourself or your relationship future: **"What is for me will not pass me."** You are still on the path of your dating destiny and every experience you've had up to this point will one day make sense in the bigger picture.

CASE STUDY: DON'T SETTLE FOR *I GUESS* WHEN YOU CAN HAVE *OF COURSE*

My client Ilene came to me after a failed six-month marriage feeling the ticking clock of biology. She wanted love, but more than anything, she wanted a child, and the age of forty was knocking at her door. She felt like a major life goal was going to pass her by if she didn't take action soon.

A few relationships came and went, then one man she dated seemed to check all of her boxes. You know . . . The List. They had passion, they had fun together, he respected her and supported her career. Yet as they stood on the brink of yet another breakup, she asked him what he thought about having kids.

It wasn't the first time she'd asked, but she knew it would be the last. His response: "I *guess* I could see myself having kids with you." Her heart sank because she knew that having kids was not a kinda, sorta, maybe situation. It was a full-court-press, all-hands-on-deck decision. It was a key element of her Goals Pillar that was not to be overlooked. They broke up, leaving her disappointed and more discouraged about her motherhood timeline than before.

I convinced Ilene to give a dating app one last try. We polished her profile at the top of the new year. By March, she met a man she fell for immediately. By the summer, they moved in together. By fall, they were engaged. Nearly a year to the day from their first date, they got married. Their daughter was born two years later and they're still madly in love.

I shudder to think what would have happened if Ilene settled for "I guess" when she could've had "of course." Her prior boyfriend showed her what was in his life plan. Even before that fateful conversation, with his words and noncommittal actions he showed her that kids were not on his immediate list of life goals. She wanted to believe that he could grow into her vision of what their life together could be. He wasn't The One. The man who is now her husband is, and his *yes* was right on the other side of the other man's *no* when she was brave enough to hear it and could step out on faith that the life she truly wanted was still out there.

So much of dating today is a leap of faith. We can't control other people's actions, sometimes we can bend their will to what we want, but at a certain point, you have to *allow*. Allowing means trusting that if you have a clear mindset on who you are and your goals for the relationship you're creating, you get out the way and give the chi a chance to flow without directing its every move. Everyone who is in love today at some point took a leap of faith.

This Dear Damona question illustrates the feelings that come up when we have clarity about our goals and express them confidently:

> *Dear Damona,*
> *I have no children, and I don't want any children. It says that on my dating profile. It also says on my profile that I do not date men with children of any age. So regardless of that, being on my profile, I still get men who disregard that. That is a nonnegotiable for me and they still match with me. Recently, I was called shallow because of that desire to date someone who doesn't have kids. Is that really being shallow? Or just stating what I need to be happy in a relationship?*

When someone else's goals aren't aligned with ours and that person isn't coming from a place of empathy, they drop their pain and disappointment on our doorstep. Just because they've sent it doesn't mean that you have to accept delivery. Mindfully choosing not to have kids is anything but shallow. The person who said that it is was responding to their own feelings of rejection for not being the right match. It's not your stuff, so you can internally return that emotion to sender.

If you relate to this question, you might want to consider, however, what having kids means to you. Sometimes we decide we don't want a certain thing in our life because of an assumption of what that thing might mean or because we're considering a life choice that could have many variables from a singular point of view. It's possible your match could have kids who are grown-up or who don't live with him. If his kids were not a part of his daily life, would that still be a deal breaker for you? What if he had children who've passed away but he, understandably, still marked his profile as having children? You would eliminate him before he's had a chance to paint a picture of his situation. Our prior experiences and impressions of imagined scenarios drive us to segment our dating pool into neat categories. As you've probably already found out or even lived through yourself, most people are a little messy and don't color inside the lines, so these rigid boxes hurt us more than they help.

Sometimes this process brings up discouragement because we know what life we want but it feels far away and unattainable to us. Even though my coaching program and the exercises in this book are designed for dating, I often find that clients can use them to improve other aspects of their lives, too, because limiting beliefs in dating are often rooted deeper in our overall limiting beliefs and residual feelings of shame, guilt, and disappointment.

Dear Damona,

How would someone with financial insecurities approach online dating? I'm 60K in debt, most of it is student loans. I'm ashamed of my debt & don't want potential partners to know. For context, I have a great stable job at a nonprofit but live in a city with a ridiculous cost of living. I always pay all my bills & rent on time. I just have this monkey on my back that I can't seem to shake & it prevents me from buying a house. When is it appropriate to reveal my financial situation to someone I'm dating?

When we look to our own future and see shame, overwhelm, and hopelessness, it no doubt impacts our confidence in dating. This letter writer is pushing away potential partners based on an assumption that matches will be scared of their debt, but that's only the letter writer's own emotional attachment to the money speaking. With postpandemic job insecurity, rising college costs, skyrocketing housing costs, and a broken healthcare system, many people are in debt today. This person is taking themselves out of the dating pool using the best-case-scenario belief that the person they meet will be debt-free and will judge their debt as harshly as this person judges it themselves.

Shifting your perspective begins with having a plan. In this person's case, it means a plan to pay down or manage their debt or reframe their thoughts about financial success. For some, just paying bills on time every month is financial success. This person is tied to the outcome of buying a house as a way of demonstrating success, but that is likely a belief that was seeded at a time when buying a house after completing college and establishing a career was the natural progression for a person. It also may have come from a time when both college and houses were more affordable. It's unfair to judge your current situation by rules and timelines of the past.

Your shame might be financial or it might come in the form of judging your body, hating your career, or fearing that your past will repeat itself. If you develop your personal goals for a more abundant future and identify a plan to get there, even if it's a twenty- or thirty-year runway, you will feel less out of control and you'll be able to communicate to your future partner about the issue in a way that doesn't bring up more shame for you.

SHOW ME THE MONEY

While we're on the topic of money, two conversations about finances frequently arise for daters. Early on, you must talk about your spending habits and discretionary income because these impact how you spend your time together. Often, when one partner makes a great deal less, they feel uncomfortable expressing how certain dates or experiences are financially unreasonable for them.

When my husband and I met, I was making nearly double his salary. He had the budget to go out only a couple of times a month and he didn't have the money to take trips together. I had a choice. I could compromise on our activities and find things we could do together that didn't cost much money or we could break up. There technically was a third option of me paying for our dates, but he was very clear that wasn't something he wanted. I'd never been a woman who needed to be wined and dined or was impressed by a date spending money, so it was obvious to me that the venue for our dates didn't matter, it was about getting to know each other better, and ultimately we came up with more creative dates because we had to carve our own path.

And don't put the cart before the horse by assuming that your debt makes you unattractive to matches. Deal with the immediate financial situation, and if things start looking serious and you begin to trust the person, then you can and should share the financial picture with them along with your plan to manage it. Debt versus immediate expenses is a relationship conversation versus a dating conversation. Your debt really only becomes your partner's problem if you get married and your assets and debts become one with theirs. Some matches will evaluate you from the beginning based on how expensive your dates are and how much discretionary income you have. Those aren't your people. Find matches who see the bigger picture and value you for everything else you bring to the relationship nonmonetarily.

Here's another question about relationship goals that seems to come up every few months for my listeners:

Dear Damona,
My dating profile states that I am looking for something more serious. I'll match with someone, they say they are looking for something more serious as well, but then by the third or fourth date they say that I am further along in wanting a commitment and they aren't quite ready for a relationship and want to keep things casual. I have ended it there because that is not what I am looking for. It has happened to me four times now. What are some signs I can look out for to avoid this happening again and is there anything I can do to find someone more serious about wanting a relationship?

This is a lesson in the Maya Angelou philosophy of "people will show you who they are the first time." Many times, clients tell me that they don't know what their partner wants or where the relationship is headed, but when I read their messages or the partner's profile I see that it's been plainly spelled out. The dissonance comes up when that person's goal isn't the same as ours and we're trying to make it fit or hope that they will change.

If from the beginning you're being transparent about your goals and giving your date a clear sense of the relationship you are building, you've done your part, but it can take a couple of dates to see whether someone is on the same page. It's not wasted time but part of the process as you demonstrate what your ideal relationship looks like and they decide whether they're up for that journey or they need to hop off at the next stop. Someone might declare that they want commitment but realize that their definition of commitment is different from yours, or they might change their mind entirely. I look at all feedback as useful, even if it doesn't get us the outcome we want with that person. It's better to know than to stay in limbo.

A girlfriend of one of my friends openly called her guy "The Egg Thief." Being in the forty-something category, she felt that his lack of commitment was stealing her potential to have children. Eventually, they broke up and within a few months he met a woman, they got pregnant, and suddenly he was married with a baby after so many months of squandering his ex's egg potential. It wasn't that he didn't want a commitment or didn't want children. It's that he didn't see a future with her and may have lacked the awareness or confidence at the time to express it. However, when his new girlfriend came into his life, his path suddenly came into focus and his new relationship goal unfolded from there.

How you proceed depends on how many eggs you want to crack open, hoping and waiting for your person to have an egg-istential awakening. Sorry, I couldn't help myself, but I think you get the point.

One last FAQ for you on deal breakers that comes up for my type A, achievement-oriented daters.

> Dear Damona,
> I have a great, well-paying job and I've been saving up to buy a house. I have had people tell me that it's a big turnoff for men, though, if I already own my own home and have a successful career. Should I wait to buy until after I've met someone?

Just imagine for a moment what it would be like to be in a partnership with someone who is intimidated by your success. Picture how great it will be to tiptoe around them when you get a promotion and what it will feel like to make yourself small so they can feel big. In case, you haven't figured it out yet, this is my sarcasm speaking. Certain people will be intimidated by your success, and those are certainly the wrong people for you to date. You should never defer your goals in another area of your life in pursuit of the possibility of love.

We are in a time of major change for gender equality. Starting in 1972 when Title IX gave more women the opportunity to go to college, ladies have been outpacing men on both enrollment and completion of college degrees, with the gap widening even more for graduate and doctoral degrees. This is great news for gender parity in the workforce but puts straight women who are seeking someone at their career or educational level at a disadvantage because there really aren't enough men to go around.

As Jon Birger, a regular *Dates & Mates* guest, suggests in his book *Date-onomics: How Dating Became a Lopsided Numbers Game*, this means that women seeking men must let go of this antiquated expectation that men must have a higher level of education and financial stability to be suitable partners. We cannot flip the equation in one area and then expect the rest of the calculation to stay the same. We have to adjust our personal expectations and then our societal norms to adapt to the changing factors.

chapter 4

F the list, fix your mindset

NOW THAT YOU UNDERSTAND HOW THE LIST MYTH COULD BE sabotaging your chances of making a match before you even get to the date and how strengthening the Goals Pillar can put you in the right mindset for dating, I want to offer you tangible steps to make this shift.

First, you have to create space for the person to arrive into your life. I'll begin with a cautionary tale of a client who struggled to clear a path for love.

CASE STUDY: I'M GOING TO LOSE YOU

We were forty minutes into our second phone session and as soon as I heard, "I'm going into the tunnel, I'm going to lose you in a sec," my heart sank. Not because I didn't want my client to hang up on me but because I didn't want my client to hang up on herself. For some time, I'd been asking clients to sign a code of conduct as a condition of beginning my program. The form requested that clients show up on time and in focus for the duration of the hour session. My program had a 90 percent success rate, which meant that most of my clients were dating someone exclusively by the end of our three-month period together. The 10 percent who slipped through my fingers broke my heart because I could have helped them too. Results come down to reframing beliefs around dating, and some people just cannot do it.

There's a moment when I can always tell whether we are going to hit a turning point or a wall, and my client "C" and I had arrived at that fork in the road. She knew her dating life was "a problem" (her words, not mine) and wanted to do something about it, so a friend suggested she reach out to me. As a corporate consultant, she loved meeting new people and having deep, thoughtful conversations, but she didn't have much free time to date. She wanted a boyfriend but loathed everything that led up to that point, including going on dates. Nevertheless, "C" was convinced that she could improve her situation simply by hiring a dating coach.

In the meantime, she'd forgotten to put our second session in the calendar and her assistant had scheduled a cross-town meeting. She asked if she could join from the car. Begrudgingly, I accepted, in spite of the fact that I knew it was hard to be introspective while rushing down the West Side Highway.

As she drove, I asked her to describe her ideal match to me. She drew a blank and replied simply, "I'll know it when I see it."

I dug in for more detail. What would he be like? Where might she potentially cross paths with him? What would he enjoy doing for fun?

She rattled off a list of things she used to enjoy doing but admitted that most of the time she just hangs out at home with her friends. "Well, if he's not the pizza delivery man, he's probably not going to show up on your doorstep," I quipped. Intellectually, she could hear what I was saying, but she was not in a place where she could really step into this experience, either physically or emotionally. "Can we picture how your life would look with this person in it?" I inquired. She stumbled to find the words as she narrated her frustration over trying to change lanes in rush-hour traffic.

"I'm going to lose you," she said as she slipped underground forty minutes into our scheduled time together. And that was it. That was our last session. I followed up a few times to get her to complete the program, but she couldn't make it work with her schedule.

When we have very full, satisfying lives, it's hard to make the space for a person you haven't met to enter into it. I hear from busy clients that they'll make the time when they meet the person, but what they fail to realize is that, statistically speaking, going to the same places and doing the same things is likely to yield the same results (in other words, no new matches). Then, even if that person were to arrive, I question whether they would feel like there is space for them in your very full life. You want that person to feel welcomed into your life, not like they're in competition with your job, your family, your hobbies, or your other priorities.

It's not always your season to find love. There are times when your career, family, or personal interests take precedence. However, if you want your life to change, space needs to be created for your process.

When you really think about it, who you choose to partner with is the most important decision you'll ever make. It affects your finances, your mental health, your family, where you live, and every single aspect of your life—yet it's the decision that is most often left to chance. Partnering is put on the back burner until the pain of not having a relationship overtakes your desire for other things or your ability to ignore the issue. If you apply the same kind of focus and give finding love the same kind of importance that you give to other areas of your life, just imagine what could be possible.

TAKE A DATING SNAPSHOT

As we begin dating in this new mindful way, it's important to memorialize where you are now. Many of the changes you will experience through unraveling your love myths will happen gradually, and sometimes down the road you forget just how far you've come.

Take a moment to capture a dating snapshot of where you are right now with relationships. I recommend keeping a journal to record your milestone moments along the way. Journaling can also help you process the thoughts and feelings that come up on this journey.

First, let's begin with the numbers. Answer the following questions in your journal.

How long has it been since your last relationship?
How many dates have you been on in the last year or the last
month?
When would you like to see yourself moving into a relationship?
Three months? Six months? A year? Longer?
What have you been doing in pursuit of a relationship thus far?

You can use your journal daily or weekly to track your changing thoughts or reach for it in those peak emotional moments to gain perspective over time. Here are some primer questions you can ask yourself regularly:

What did I do today in pursuit of my ideal relationship?
Who/what did I give my time and energy to today?
Where do I want to put my energy tomorrow?
What did I learn about myself today?
What question about myself do I hope to answer tomorrow or in
the future?

I ask my clients to answer one final question, either in their journal or internally, every day.

What am I grateful for today?

That final question is important when we are in pursuit of something new because it helps us move forward not from a place of lack but from a place of abundance. You likely already have your basic needs met. Reminding yourself of the abundance in your life right now, even if it doesn't include a romantic relationship, will help you date from a place of fullness. You can open your heart and your life to someone new because you already have everything you need to feel secure. You want a relationship, but it helps to see it as additive to your already full life, not filling a hole of something that is missing.

ADOPT AN ATTITUDE OF YES

To allow a shift into our lives, we must embrace an expansive attitude and a willingness to change entrenched patterns and to grow. I call this adopting an attitude of yes.

This attitude encompasses an overall openness to new experiences and a positive outlook on the future. It also can mean saying yes to things that you otherwise might have said no to.

If a person invites you to a party and you won't know anyone, say yes.

If you get a chance to do a unique activity, say yes.

If you have an opportunity to go on a completely blind date set up by a friend? That's a yes too!

When you allow more "yes" into your life, it paves the way for a yes in the relationship that you want.

To get a different outcome, you have to shake up your normal patterns. So, the next time you get an opportunity that may seem a little out of the box for you, get curious about what might happen if you say yes instead of an automatic no.

REWRITING YOUR STORY

Rather than going into your dating app and simply checking the same boxes you've always checked for traits you seek in a partner (incidentally the same boxes that other people are generally ticking off too), let's lead with your heart instead of your head.

We are all the sum of our experiences. You have had experiences in your life that have led to particular beliefs about yourself, about your worthiness, and about your ability to find the right match. You have an opportunity today to rewrite that. Every day you have a chance to start fresh, and what has been your story about love doesn't have to be your story any longer. It all begins with shifting beliefs and taking action to create room for your new story to be written. It might not read like a fairy tale, but when you're intentional about creating your story, it's actually a far more interesting journey.

DATING SAMSKARAS

Yogis call our deeply ingrained patterns *samskaras*. This term comes from the Sanskrit words *sam*, meaning "well planned out," and *kara*, meaning "action, cause, or doing." Samskaras reside in the unconscious self and form the basic inner drives that influence and affect future actions. They are like seeds that have been planted in your subconscious brain that eventually sprout into the actions you take.

Brain science supports this concept that we are forging new paths in our mind with every choice and belief we hold. The human brain is made up of an estimated one hundred billion neurons that make a total of a hundred trillion neural connections. When you engage in practices that increase feelings of happiness and a vision of the happy relationship you want, you increase activity in your prefrontal cortex, the part of the brain that influences personality, decision-making, and planning for the future. The more you practice, the more neurons that fire and the more you strengthen brain pathways that make it easier to replicate those feelings of happiness. People who are optimistic have more activity in their left prefrontal cortex than people who are pessimistic. I'm not suggesting that we all just live in a fantasy land of happiness and visualization of the future, but I do see a direct correlation between identifying which negative thoughts are impacting your choices and which positive ones can be fortified and transformed into new neural pathways of possibility.

I call limiting beliefs about love *dating samskaras*. When you are unaware of them, you bring them with you on every date, and they trail behind like a safety blanket. To cut the cord, you need to take decisive action. That begins with acknowledging these unconscious imprints and rewriting them and rewiring your thoughts to set a new path for yourself.

It's not all doom and gloom. There are both pleasurable and painful samskaras. For every belief that is negatively affecting your life, you have the power to form new beliefs. Those beliefs will become different habits that net a different outcome throughout your life but especially in love.

Here's a samskara exercise to get you started. Complete the following phrase with the first thing that comes to mind:

> *I have not found my ideal match yet because* _____.

Don't judge whatever comes into your mind; first, simply observe it.

Now, imagine for just a moment that what you wrote is not actually true. Your prior experiences all layered together to create a narrative that you were convinced to believe. These thoughts drove a groove in your mind, like a well-worn path or a scar: a samskara. But are they factual? Or are they simply beliefs that you have fortified with your thoughts? You have the power to carve a new belief for yourself today by rerouting that mental traffic.

Let's reexamine that belief you had about why you haven't found your person yet and create a new script. What would the inverse of your statement be?

- I'm meeting quality matches everywhere I go.
- There are many great matches in my area.
- I'm learning how to be loved and I'm growing every day.

Or even:

- I'm in a loving relationship with my person.

As preposterous as it might seem now because you are still looking for this person, once you meet them, it will feel just as ridiculous that you ever had that original belief. I know this because the life I've built felt unattainable to me at one point, and yet I'm here today living it.

In feng shui, yogic philosophy, the law of attraction, and many other modalities, a key element is to visualize the new future as if it is already happening. Saying "I *will* have a romantic relationship" always places the vision in the future. To fully bring it into reality, in your mind picture it as if it's happening now.

The same neurons fire in our brain whether we are visualizing a particular reality or actually living it. Studies have shown that people who imagine themselves flexing a muscle can actually get stronger without doing any physical movement. This is part of the reason elite athletes like Michael Phelps and Tiger Woods regularly use visualization to improve their performance. Science has shown that thought-work can actually strengthen the brain *and* the body.

To reprogram your mental computer, you must see your old phrase as a trigger. Every time it pops up in your mind, you first observe that it's happening again, then replace it mentally with the inverse statement. I suggest creating a simple transition word or sound that signals to you that the negative samskara is back. I like to say, "Ding," like there's a bell going off in my head, to tell me to change scripts and repeat the positive samskara in my mind. You could use the words *no, aha,* and even *thank you* when you catch yourself falling into the old pattern and need to remember your positive phrase instead.

Refocusing your thoughts is the quickest way to shift your mindset and therefore your actions as well. You don't need to believe it fully at first. Just pick a positive phrase that you view as at least 51 percent possible. Choose an outcome that you believe is slightly more probable than not. Perhaps you don't see that it could be true today or tomorrow, but you believe it could unfold at some time in the future. By doing this, you're planting a seed for something new to blossom. You're preparing your body and mind for the moment when you meet your person so your nervous system will know what to do.

At the beginning, you might encounter your negative samskara twenty or thirty times in a day. Try not to judge that either. This is likely a deeply ingrained belief that will take time to unravel. Awareness is the first step to making a change.

As you move through this process of strengthening your Four Pillars, stay mindful of how this experience–thought–action cycle is shifting for you. Eventually, you will see that your destiny is not already written, your experience can and will be different, but it all begins with your own mindset.

OUT WITH CHECKING BOXES

Checking boxes never really suited me. From the time I was born, I have always seemed to live just outside the lines. The first time I became aware of this, I was staring at a standardized test form in elementary school. I knew the material backward and forward, but I couldn't get past the cover page of the test. First name. Last name. Gender. Race (check one). I scanned the list: Caucasian, African American, Native American, Asian/Pacific Islander, Hispanic. How could there be only five boxes? Why did I have to check only one?

If I chose one box, I would be denying one parent and half of my identity. If I just checked Caucasian, did that really convey the nuance of my father's Jewish religion and our culture? If I just checked African American, it would satisfy the quizzical looks that screamed "What is she?" but completely negate my close relationship with my father. I stared at the page as it stared back at me. *Check one.*

"Fill the circles in completely," my teacher reminded us. "And don't leave any question blank." So, I poured my heart and soul into that first question. Beginning with a single sentence, my thoughts began to flow into the margin and down the side of the cover page. By the time I was finished, my graphite tip had been worn down to a nub.

I refused to be reduced to a box. Even at nine years old, I knew that the world was changing and I couldn't just go along with the status quo. I had faith that there were others like me out there. Maybe their skin didn't look like mine, maybe they didn't go to temple, but there were other misfits who didn't fit into society's predetermined boxes.

Humans are far less genetically diverse across races than other mammals are within species. Most of us are a mix of multiple cultures and nationalities. We are more similar than we are different. Now here we find ourselves on dating apps sorting people into boxes again in an effort to shortcut our road to human connection. You can check all the boxes you want: height, sports and hobbies, income, age, but in the end, those boxes can't tell you who someone is. And you don't have to check just one box anymore.

Much like the exercise I did with my feng shui consultant all those years ago, I'd like for you to visualize this new life you're building and the person you are building it with, beyond boxes.

EXERCISE: GOALS FOR THE FUTURE

To go from a finite list mindset to an expansive goals-driven mindset, we first need clarity on where we are headed and the timeline on which we hope to achieve those milestones.

Here are some prompts to get you started. You can write the answers in your journal:

> *When you picture your ideal relationship, what does it look like?*
> *Where are you in your career path? Where do you want to be?*
> *What resources do you both need to support your finances, goals, and the future life you're building?*
> *Do you see yourself remaining in your current town or city?*
> *Where would you go if you had the freedom to live anywhere?*
> *What do you hope you'll accomplish in your lifetime?*
> *What do you want more of in your life?*
> *What do you want to release from your life entirely?*

You can take this process a step further by going through a visualization exercise. I find that simply listing your goals can keep some people in a list mindset but *feeling* your relationship goals and how you want to experience your next relationship will put you on a path to bringing it to life the way it did for me during the feng shui practice.

IDEAL MATE VISUALIZATION

Imagine that you are walking up to the door of your home. When you get there, the door is opened by a familiar face—it's you but five years in the future (you look fabulous, by the way).

Future You sits Current You down at the table and describes your new life. You hear all of the fabulous things that Future You and Your Future Partner are doing together and how great this life you've built is.

What does your home look like?

Who else is there? Are there children? Other family members? Are there pets?

What do you and your partner love doing together?

How do you show love for one another?

How has this relationship changed you?

What is the same?

*How do you feel being with this person?**

Pay attention to the details that really light you up and excite you. Everything that Future You is sharing is possible in this vision. It feels visceral, tangible, and thrilling.

---

* There is a recorded audio visualization for this on my website Damona Hoffman.com.

Thank Future You for sharing your story and picture yourself walking away invigorated by the exciting life that's waiting right around the corner.

THE VISION BOARD

Once you have a clear vision of your relationship goals, you can create a physical representation of them to provide a constant touchstone to remind you of what you want and deserve in a relationship.

I believe vision boards work for more than esoteric reasons. They stimulate your reticular activating system, the filters in your brain that help you know what's important to pay attention to and what can be ignored. This enables you to notice the people and choices that are in alignment with your relationship goals, and having ongoing contact with those visuals makes you more likely to recognize the traits you desire when you see them out in the world. A visual reminder that a relationship is important to you can also keep you motivated even when you feel that you're losing dating momentum.

You can use many apps and online resources to create a digital vision board, but I like the tactile process of making them the old-fashioned way, with magazines. I've actually led several vision board workshops over the last decade and I always keep a stack of magazines at the ready in case a vision board opportunity presents itself. Here is my process:

First, you need a piece of posterboard, scissors, glue, and a stack of magazines. Then:

1. **Scan for images.** Flip through magazines to see which images jump out at you. Especially if you do this step after a visualization, your brain is primed to pick up the most important markers. If you don't find what you're looking for in magazines, you can always do an online search for the image that you want and print it (assuming it's just for your personal use and not violating any copyright laws).

2. **Seek out words or phrases.** Many of my clients find they are motivated by inspiring phrases and words. Look for those words to show up as you're scanning magazines or you can purchase stickers or scrapbooking materials with affirmations. You can even stitch thoughts together if you see the words you want in different phrases. Or write your guiding phrases with a marker.

3. **Assemble.** Some people like to paste their elements as they go. I do my board in phases and in the end arrange all the pieces before I start to attach them. Sometimes words or images don't make the cut, so if I wait to paste until I can see everything on the board together, I won't have to paste over anything.

When your board is complete, you have a physical picture of the life and romance that you imagine for yourself. Place it somewhere that you can view it daily as a constant road map to the life you're building. When your partner comes into your life, you might even want to share it with them as a conversation starter to clarify the direction of the relationship. If they're into it, you could create a new couples vision board with them.

TRADE THE LIST MYTH FOR A BRIGHTER FUTURE

Our fear of rejection overshadows our ability to express what we truly want in a relationship. Without doing a deeper dive into our needs and focusing our minds on a relationship goal, we revert to unconscious programming. Playing it safe in our relationship expectations is evolutionarily preferred. If we stick with what we know, we can better predict the outcome. Yet you've seen from the exercises in this book that allowing yourself to dream and stretching what you think is possible for your relationship future are thrilling. Not only thrilling but possible.

You might not recognize the packaging that love comes in, but you will recognize that feeling when it's repeated. You will know when you feel safe, seen, and supported because the feeling that arose in your visualization will appear again. When you begin from a place of clarity about the future, you'll be amazed at how easy it is to recognize the person who stimulates the feelings you experienced when you imagined your relationship future. The second-guessing of matches who fit your list criteria but don't speak to your soul will disappear and you'll be able to get to a deeper level of connection and clarity more quickly.

To reach the relationship we dream of, we have to step into the unknown. There's a lot of fear out there. But risking and moving past fear are what get you to the reward of love.

Dear Damona,

I'm having trouble feeling confident and attractive to men. I do affirmations and positive self-talk, but I still let my fear of rejection hold me back. I have had zero luck when I approach a man first and then down goes my confidence. I'm fifty-five and I just feel invisible most of the time.

When you approach someone, your confidence cannot be tied to the outcome of the encounter. This letter writer has to break the connection to the ending of the story she's told herself so many times about why approaching a man gets her zero luck. I hear from a lot of older women who feel invisible because our society traditionally promotes youth as beauty, but folks are catching on that this narrative is false, and it's time this letter writer did too.

If you let go of wanting to control what happens when you approach someone, what happens to your fear? If fear was not there, what would you do differently? What would you say and how would you say it? If you let go of your fear and said what was in your heart without any attachment to their response, could it work in reverse and actually boost your confidence level?

Dating with purpose is not about how many people you can get to pursue you; it's about getting to a more honest place about who you are and how you want to live your life. Remember, it takes only one person to turn your relationship reality around, so try not to get too invested in any one match when you send that first message. I always say on *Dates & Mates*, treat those messages and matches like coins in a fountain. If you toss in a penny and your wish comes true, that's a beautiful blessing, but if it doesn't, are you really going to be disappointed over a penny? Toss more pennies, make more wishes, and the ones that are meant to come true will.

If you've dated by list in the past, hopefully you're now seeing possibility in a new way of dating. You should be leaving The Mindset phase with a clear idea of the life that you see yourself building with a partner. We are our thoughts. Thoughts build a path for our beliefs, our actions, and our future. So, as Oprah Winfrey once said, "Create the highest, grandest vision possible for your life because you become what you believe."

THE MINDSET ACTION STEPS

1. *Visualize the love life you want.* Try meditation, vision board-ing, or writing down your new love story to give you a clear picture of your relationship goals.

2. *Identify your must-haves and deal breakers.* Using life goals as the lens, identify what you must have in a relationship and what you cannot live with.

3. *Take a dating snapshot.* Memorialize where you are in the dat-ing process right now so you can track the changes in your dating life after you complete the steps in this book.

4. *Reframe your dating samskaras.* Become aware of your limit-ing beliefs and rewire your brain for the loving relationship that you will soon build.

part II

the search

chapter 5

the rules myth

ONCE UPON A TIME, THERE WAS A HUMBLE MAN WHO WISHED to woo the heart of a lady. She would be impressed by no ordinary man. He would have to prove his valor by slaying the dragon, climbing the wall, giving her True Love's kiss, or any number of ridiculous steps to show he was worthy. Honestly, the man was pretty tired of following the rules because it seemed that, as soon as he completed his challenges, the rules changed and new challenges were set before him. It's all because he was following the wrong rules and trying to win the wrong maidens.

Enter stage left: the Rules Myth. The bad news is the Rules Myth keeps many people from finding a connection because either they have no idea what to do in dating or they have limited their options by following rules others have written. But the good news is rules were made to be broken.

I entered the dating industry at a time when the concept of a dating coach was foreign to most people. Hiring a consultant to help you launch a business? Smart. Going to therapy if your marriage was on the rocks? Of course. But paying a professional to guide you along the dynamic and ever-changing road to love? Unfathomable. All we knew was *The Rules*, *The Game*, and *The Bachelor*.

The Rules is a book written in 1995 by Ellen Fein and Sherrie Schneider that outlines a specific set of commandments that, when followed precisely, give female readers the promise of "capturing the heart of Mr. Right." When it was released, this book set the world on fire. Not because the concepts were so revolutionary (the book itself touts the tips as time-tested secrets) but because it was one of the first modern books to spell out a series of steps that demystified this grand question of how to fall in love. And thus, "don't talk to a man first," "don't meet him halfway," and over two dozen other rules became nonnegotiable protocol for achieving "success"—defined as a marriage proposal.

The rules made many women see "getting the ring" as a game they had to play if they wanted to win a good life. I appreciate that *The Rules* was one of the first books and philosophies that indicated to women that they didn't have to stand by as a lady-in-waiting for love. But I'm less enthusiastic about the cold, robotic calculation that comes along with strictly following *The Rules*. It turns some ladies into used car salesmen who talk a big game but know that once the car leaves the lot, it can't be returned. Once the ring is on, the mask comes down and we're left with the harsh reality of hasty matrimonial choices. *The Rules* turned dating into

a chess game with one-size-fits-all moves that ignore the importance of introspection and finding a match that is uniquely suited
for you.

Then along came men's answer to *The Rules*. In the 2005 book
The Game, Neil Strauss embedded himself in the pickup artist community, a subculture of dating coaching that has long
existed, the ethics of which I have long debated on my podcast.
Pickup artists, known in the business as PUAs, teach men techniques to manipulate a certain outcome with women. Strauss,
who originally observed "The Game" as a journalist, got so
sucked up into the system that he followed it up with a second
book, *Rules of the Game*. Then he wrote another book called *The
Truth: An Uncomfortable Book About Relationships*, which outlines
his challenges in relationships after being immersed in the PUA
world. *The Game* convinced men that there is a secret formula
to follow to achieve "success" with women in the form of sexual
desirability and limitless confidence.

One evening about ten years ago, I was at a party at a famous
influencer's house. He had gathered a handful of collaborators
and friends for an evening of business networking. When I
arrived, I was slightly intimidated to find over forty men in atten-
dance and only about three women. Still, as an extrovert, I figured I wouldn't have a problem making new friends.

Midway through the party, I found myself standing next to an
average-looking guy in his twenties. His pants are best described
as unnecessarily embellished and too tight in all the wrong
places. His dirty blond hair was swooped to the side just so. He
was not someone who would have caught my eye when I was single. We began talking and he asked what I did for a living.

"I'm a dating coach," I replied. Much to my surprise, he said, "I'm a dating coach too." I thought we were going to have a fascinating conversation about our strategies, our clients, or all the things we had in common, but instead he snapped back, "If you're a dating coach, how come I don't know you?" My first instinct was to recite my résumé in an effort to prove that I was, in fact, a legitimate dating coach. I stopped myself when the inverse question crossed my mind: If he was a dating coach, how come I didn't know him?

He went on to boast about his many accolades and accomplishments, all the while trying to undermine me and make me question my own experience. Then it dawned on me that he was not actually a dating coach. He was a PUA and I had fallen victim to one of the most common strategies in the PUA playbook—negging.

Negging: An act of emotional manipulation whereby a person makes a deliberate backhanded compliment, thinly veiled insult, or otherwise cheeky remark in an effort to undermine their mark's confidence and increase their need for the manipulator's approval.

This was textbook negging, and even as a dating coach, I almost fell into the trap. An entire generation of men were conditioned to believe that this was an effective strategy to get a woman's self-confidence low enough that she would fall for them, even if they were running on self-esteem fumes themselves.

Men attended workshops, retreats, online courses, and "in the field" trainings to learn how to employ these borderline sociopathic techniques to get dates. The worst part is that they actually worked for a while. Back when meeting people at bars and parties was the predominant avenue for connecting, negging worked like a charm. It happens so fast, it's easy to get caught up in the momentum. Of course, now with apps being the primary way to meet a dating prospect, negging is a little harder to pull off, because a manipulative ploy over text will surely be screenshotted and turned into a viral TikTok video. However, the lasting legacy of pickup artist culture remains and continues to trick us into a dishonest approach to meeting potential partners.

The Rules Myth is in the driver's seat for daters of all genders. My inbox is full of questions about dos and don'ts, timelines and strategies. How do you play the game as efficiently as possible without breaking too much of a sweat? How far will you go to get the relationship you want?

For me, this myth conjures images of Cinderella's stepsisters trying to squeeze into that dainty little slipper to get the prince. In the original Grimm Cinderella tale, Driselda even sawed off her toes in an effort to get the shoe to fit. She was so desperate to fool the prince into taking her instead of Cinderella that she was willing to leave herself bloody and permanently disfigured. Which parts of yourself have you been willing to lop off and leave behind in the hopes of being more suitable or lovable?

I imagine you were expecting more romantic images in a dating book. We'll get to your romantic ending, but first we have to unravel the ugly truth that has led us here. I say F the fairy tale. We have to be willing to peer into those dark places in the basement of our hearts and shine a little light around to see what has kept us from experiencing the kind of love we deserve. We have to write our own love story.

GET THE ROSE

Nothing exemplifies the concepts of *The Rules* and *The Game* better than *The Bachelor*. Created in 2002, the show is essentially a beauty contest on steroids. It was the first reality show to gamify the experience of finding lasting love, and they upped the ante by making the contestants actually live with the others who were dating the same person of their dreams. It captured our hearts by leaning into a concept that we'd already bought into: dating is a game, and you compete with other Bachelors and Bachelorettes for the heart of your betrothed. If you are strategic enough and apply the rules in your favor, you could win at the game of love.

The feminist in me loathes this concept, but my reality TV producer roots know precisely why this show is so addictive, has birthed many spinoffs, and is one of the longest-running reality TV shows in history. We want to believe that if we play by the rules, we, too, can orchestrate our own happily ever after. If this were true, I imagine more of the "winning" couples would still be together. Instead, once they get the ring and leave the pressure cooker of competition for the realities of building a relationship, the illusion is shattered.

I had the opportunity to dissect this experience on *Dates & Mates* with Nick Viall, one of the only people to appear on all of the Bachelor Nation shows: *The Bachelor*, *The Bachelorette* (twice), and *Bachelor in Paradise*.

After another public *Bachelor* breakup, the dating game changed for him when his girlfriend slid into his DMs. A bold action that flies in the face of *The Rules*, *The Game*, and most prior dating codes of conduct that said a woman can't make the first move. Yet the next thing he knew, a long weekend together in New York inspired a longer relationship than in his many attempts to find love on the show.

A REVEAL ABOUT GENDER

We can't talk about *The Bachelor* without talking about gender roles. *The Bachelor* was created based on long-standing beliefs around gender that have undergone a dramatic shift over the twenty years of the show's existence.

For centuries, women had little to no choice when it came to mate selection. Up through the 1950s, your parents and your community were primarily responsible for choosing who you would spend your life with. Love was a business transaction.

It's become popular to complain about the stressors of finding love today and to lean into the overwhelm that comes with having so many dating options, but any day of the week I'd take having a choice over having my life dictated to me. We forget that choice in itself is a privilege.

Every time we make a choice, though, we expend energy. We are exhausted because we're working too hard just to stay in the same place. It can seem like the quest for love is never-ending, and ultimately, the reward may be a disappointing date or, worse yet, an unsolicited dick pic. It's hard to justify continuing an exhaustive search when you've yet to see your labor bear fruit.

Our hunter-gatherer predecessors used to spend all day tracking prey and gathering provisions for their group. A successful hunt involved a great deal of strategy and learning from the hunts that came before. It required persistence. It required an intense need to succeed. Modern life has zapped us of so many of these qualities. You no longer need a partner to be accepted into society and you may not need them for financial stability. So why bother? When anything can come to you with the tap of an app, how much persistence do you need to employ in your love life?

The repetition of phrases like "Love will happen when you least expect it" has conditioned us to think that having a plan or strategy to find love is unromantic. We'd rather read *The Rules* or play *The Game* for the promise of a quick fix, but that just perpetuates the fairy tale. Instead, we are crafting an epic love story and that takes time, focus, and patience. Of all the successes you have achieved in your life, how many of them occurred by chance? How many times did an opportunity fall in your lap overnight? We work hard and strategize in most areas of our lives, but in love, we hope we'll be lucky (or, at least, get lucky).

DO YOU WANT TO GET LUCKY?

If you've told yourself you're unlucky in love, you must rewrite that narrative. We can create our own luck. Luck is a combination of skill and perspective plus timing, but there are concrete things you can do to improve your odds. For over ten years, experimental psychologist Richard Wiseman studied the differences between people who identified themselves as either lucky or unlucky. He found that lucky people weren't just inherently lucky; they generated their own good fortune using similar principles.

First, lucky people are observant. He handed four hundred study participants a newspaper and asked them to count the photos. The people who identified themselves as unlucky took far longer to count the photos. Why? Not because they were slower at completing the task but because he'd printed on the second page: "Stop counting—There are 43 photographs in this newspaper." Those who classified themselves as lucky were far more likely to notice. Those who felt they were unlucky typically did not.

Next, he observed that those who considered themselves lucky relied on their intuition and seemed to have a positive outlook. In particular, the lucky people were resilient and bounced back quickly from anything seen as bad luck by transforming it into good luck with a shift in perspective.

Wiseman turned his findings into a "Luck School" in which he taught these luck-boosting skills and gave participants exercises to help them become more aware of details, develop positivity, and reframe bad luck. Eighty percent of the people who attended his Luck School reported feeling luckier by the end of the course. Some had work promotions fall into their lap and many said they found romance through chance encounters.

But were those encounters really serendipity? I'd say not. I believe that luck is created, as Wiseman observed, by listening to your inner compass, keeping a positive outlook, and paying attention to details. I would add that the final ingredient to the secret sauce of luck is taking strategic risks in support of your goals. Faith is not enough. You have to take action to make the magic work for you. Employing these steps, I've guided people who haven't dated in years to find their person within a matter of months or even weeks.

Although I can help my clients develop a strategy to optimize their dating app success, a key element differentiates my approach from a pickup artist's or going the route of *The Rules*.

For a deeper relationship to develop, you have to have a clear sense of your values and use that as a primary filter for anyone you want to date long term.

CASE STUDY: COUPLES THAT RIDE TOGETHER

Annette had all her ducks in a row. She had a successful career, owned a beautiful home, and the son she raised as a single mom was off to college. It was time for her to focus on herself. She'd lost 115 pounds, had some new photos taken, and told me she was feeling a newfound sense of self-worth. Annette was laser-focused on finding lasting love, and after more than a decade of singlehood and failed experiences on apps and with matchmakers, she was feeling more self-confident than ever and came to me for a new approach.

As we talked in her sessions, I got an impression of the goals and values that were important to her. Next, I needed to understand how she wanted to feel with her match. She'd just bought a motorcycle to ride into this exciting new phase of life. She was excited about exploring biker culture and finding people to ride with. Though a motorcycle might seem like a casual interest to some or just a possession to others, to Annette it indicated a lifestyle that she was stepping into. It was freedom, it was adrenaline, it was someone to ride the open road with.

My secret weapon in online dating strategy is a keyword search (well, it was a secret until a few seconds ago). Searching profiles for keywords that matter to you generally yields better matches than relying on the app's algorithm. The challenge with the popular swipe apps is that you have little control over the matching algorithm. You have to change your preferences in order to adjust your app pool.

On OkCupid, Match, and a few other apps, you can still use keywords to filter based on other factors than just the traditional age, location, and basic biographical information. Most people set those fields and forget them and then get frustrated when doing the same search again and again yields few matches or starts to repeat the same profiles after a while.

For Annette, I conducted a keyword search for "motorcycle" and pinned three or four options of men for her to consider who were bikers or were interested in motorcycles. One of those men wrote to her. They agreed to meet, and before long, they were dating exclusively. Less than eighteen months from the time Annette and I began working together, she married her sweetheart.

Here's the craziest part: they had gone to the same high school but were five years apart, never attending at the same time. They had worked for the same company in different divisions, and he lived only five miles away. Her dream partner was right under her nose her entire life, but it wasn't until their goals aligned that they found each other. Then as they got to know each other, they found that the pursuit of a similar lifestyle also corresponded to similar values and a complementary outlook on the world.

This is where the dating strategy plot thickens. As we covered in the mindset section, you must begin with clarifying your goals for the future and the life that you see yourself building. The next question that will help you navigate the next phase is: Why do you value achieving those goals? This is where the Values Pillar comes in.

chapter 6

the values pillar

WE CLING TO RULES BECAUSE THEY GIVE US A SENSE OF certainty: that's how it has always been done, so that's just how it always will be. Yet we are at a time in history when we're finally able to question some of the rules and norms that we've accepted on everything, from the way we take care of the earth to race relations. That questioning drives us to examine who we are and what we believe about the world. In that self-inquiry, we discover our core values—the beliefs and choices that govern the way we live our individual lives. When we have clear values that drive our actions, we don't need to rely on someone else telling us what we should do. That is precisely what makes the Values Pillar the antidote to the Rules Myth.

THE SEARCH FOR SHORTCUTS

Values are the primary filter in searching for a match. When I speak of values, I mean the way that you look at the world, how you choose to spend your time, and how you live your life on a day-to-day basis. Values can often be hard to decipher. As a society, we are constantly looking for shortcuts that can easily compute what someone believes.

Religion is a shortcut. We often make the assumption that if someone shares the same religious upbringing as us, they must hold the same values as us. Yet you can see, just from visiting a neighbor's church or temple, that things are done a little differently in every house of worship.

In my religion of Judaism, there are three major denominations: Orthodox, Conservative, and Reform, as well as many subsects. Someone who is Orthodox will likely observe certain rituals, such as walking instead of driving on the Sabbath and avoiding shellfish, whereas someone who is Reform might not (even though their rabbi probably told them to). The way you eat and how you connect to a higher power definitely impact how compatible you are with someone who holds a different belief system. So although you both might fall into one larger category, such as Jewish, Christian, college-educated, or family-oriented, that can mean vastly different things about your values and how you apply them to your life.

Surely political affiliation is an indication of values, right? Well, it's complicated. Although it's hard to encapsulate the totality of someone's beliefs into "red" or "blue," what is undeniable is that this factor is becoming weighted more heavily in the dating search process. In my fifteen years of coaching singles, I've seen politics go from the fifth or sixth most important quality in a match to the first or second must-have on my clients' profiles. As our views have splintered into factions based on the information we consume and believe to be true, we have come to understand political affiliation as a marker of someone's beliefs and values and have walled off into our own belief silos.

In 2016, my friend, matchmaker Maria Avgitidis Pyrgiotakis (known on Instagram as @MatchmakerMaria), appeared on *Dates & Mates* to discuss how difficult it had become to match the Trump-supporting men who engaged her services in New York City because most of the women in the dating pool had emphatically declared that they could not date anyone who voted for him. Over three million people on OkCupid said they could not date someone who had strong political beliefs that were opposite theirs.

Even a decade or two ago, couples of varied political beliefs were able to find enough common ground to coexist and fall in love, but now, not only is it a deal breaker when someone has a different political affiliation, but also people are drawing finer lines even within the same political party.

Writing for the *Washington Post*'s Date Lab column, I get to see this firsthand. Considering that much of the matchmaking pool either works in politics or is simply steeped in politics by living in DC, it's common to see matchmaking applications with a strong political preference, usually phrased as "NO Trump supporters" or "Conservatives only."

In the case of one match, the woman had worked in progressive politics for years and served on both the Hillary Clinton and the Kamala Harris campaign staffs. She was matched with a man who defined himself as a political moderate, identified himself as a fan of Andrew Yang's policies, but did not vote in the 2020 primary.

They ended the date with her on the fence about whether or not to accept a second date, so for clarification, she texted him a question that seemed innocent enough: "What do you think about Andrew Yang as an NYC mayoral candidate?"

He answered in the most honest and neutral way possible, yet she still nixed a second date, citing that he did not seem progressive enough for her. His hypothetical support of a Democratic candidate in a race in which neither of them could actually vote was the last straw.

Opposites definitely do not attract on the measure of politics. Only 21 percent of people marry someone of a different political affiliation, and most of those matches are a partisan person pairing with an independent. When we are talking Republican with Democrat, that number is only 4 percent, according to the American Family Survey.

Rather than blanketing your dating profile with statements like "Liberals Only," you can say more by signifying your values in nuanced ways. My client Kelly told me she loved watching MSNBC, so we used that detail in her profile, and although that repelled the Tucker Carlson fans, it attracted someone who was thrilled to debate Rachel Maddow's lead story with her every night. Since the 2016 election, there has been a 138 percent increase in OkCupid users saying they enjoy having political conversations. The days of avoiding politics on first dates are long over.

Other clients of mine have connected with potential dates at political rallies, while canvassing for candidates, and at fundraiser events, so if politics are that important to you, get involved and you might get a date out of it too. However, you have to ask yourself whether politics needs to be your primary values filter or you are assuming that a shared political affiliation means you'll always agree.

THE FAMILIARITY PRINCIPLE

Understanding the science of attraction is key to understanding why some people pique your interest and others fall outside of your definition of attractiveness.

In social psychology, the familiarity principle, clinically known as the mere-exposure effect, shows that humans develop a preference for things to which they are regularly exposed. We are attracted to what is familiar to us, and repeated exposure to certain people and things increases our attraction to them.

Social psychologist Robert Zajonc is the most prominent voice on the mere-exposure effect. In his research, he observed that exposure to a new and novel stimulus initially elicits a fear or avoidance response in all organisms. Each subsequent exposure to the stimulus causes less fear and more interest in the observing organism. After repeated exposure, the observing organism begins to react fondly to the once-novel stimulus.

This explains why someone can declare a preference in dating that they cannot articulate and do not really understand. They have an attraction to particular qualities because those are the faces, experiences, mannerisms, and behaviors to which they have been regularly exposed.

However, I have experienced that with time and repeated exposure, like in Zajonc's work, people become more open to expanding their dating preferences.

THE BIG DIVIDE

There's one similarity that many of my clients default to without much thought: race. This one is tricky because the beliefs around it are so deeply ingrained in our society and family of origin. But if we don't talk about it, nothing will change, and because unpacking these often unconscious beliefs can be uncomfortable, you might be cutting yourself off from someone who is an ideal match for you.

Dear Damona,
This guy I've been dating for a while is Black, and my parents are pretty racist. We aren't exclusive yet, and I don't know how to tell my parents. He has great grades and future goals. I just want my parents to approve because I really like him.

It takes tremendous bravery to step out of the norms and expectations that your parents were forced to swallow as truth. We may know that someone's race doesn't impact the kind of partner they would be, but unfortunately, our parents or grandparents may be up against experiences and beliefs that don't allow them to think the way we do. The biggest lesson here is that you cannot make your parents—or anyone else, for that matter—feel a certain way or approve of your actions. You can choose partners your parents will like, but ultimately, you are the only person who has to live your life and choose your relationships.

If you can accept that you might face a lot of discomfort from your parents and community for your choices, I believe following your heart is one of the most courageous things you can do. Whether it's race, education, income, or religion, the question is always, What kind of life do you want to build? You have to decide whether the pros of your relationship outweigh the cons, but if you go in seeking approval from your parents or your community, you'll always be chasing happiness rather than living in it.

EXPANDING OUR UNDERSTANDING

If you cannot walk a mile in someone's shoes, it is easiest to have empathy for them when you can walk a mile alongside them.

This is why a conversation around race has been a part of my coaching program since I began writing dating profiles in 2005. However, I was shocked to learn recently that many other dating coaches never touch the third rail of race. In a private Facebook group with other coaches and matchmakers I respect and trust, the question was raised, "Is it racist if someone excludes a particular race in their dating preferences?"

To me, the answer is glaringly obvious. As I said on *The Daily Show* podcast, *Beyond the Scenes*, if you are intentionally excluding one group of people based on their culture or the color of their skin, that is quite literally the definition of racism. Trust me, I referred back to the Urban Dictionary just to make sure the meaning of *racism* had not changed.

Yet I was shocked to learn that others didn't share my perspective and wrote it off, calling it a dating preference, attraction, and other coded words that cover up uncomfortable beliefs on the superiority of some races over others.

Not a good fit.

Not my type.

Has nothing in common with me.

Isn't attractive to me.

These are just some of the ways clients have attempted to brush off the question of race. Fortunately, as a dating coach, it's my business to dig deeper.

THE FIVE WHYS

As they begin my program, I always question my clients about their preferences and develop an image of their ideal mate. It is easy to influence singles to expand their ideals on height, income, education, and other factors limiting their dating pool, but whenever we get to the question of race, I hit a roadblock.

When you bring up racial preference, many people become tense and automatically assume a defensive position. I never pass judgment on clients' preferences, but as a dating coach, it is my job to help you understand your choices and examine how well they line up with your actual beliefs and the goals you wish to achieve.

As clients struggled to articulate why they felt a certain way about a certain race, it dawned on me that a popular business technique called the Five Whys could be effective in the dating coaching setting as well.

The Five Whys is a technique developed in the 1930s by Saki-chi Toyoda, founder of Toyota Industries. It became popular in the 1970s, and Toyota still uses it to solve business challenges today.

The method is surprisingly simple: when you have a problem to solve or a question to answer, you start by asking, *Why?* Each answer is followed up with another query: *Why?* Once you answer why five times, you generally get to the root cause of a belief or challenge, or you realize that the original question does not hold as much value as the client thought it did at the beginning.

Here's an example of how this conversation might go.

Me: I noticed on your dating profile that you checked an interest in White, Hispanic, and Asian, but not Black. Why?

Client: I've just never been attracted to Black men.

Me: Why do you think that is?

Client: I don't know. I suppose I've just never dated someone Black before.

Me: But why?

Client: Well, I don't know that many Black people. There aren't many Black people at work or in my neighborhood.

Me: I wonder why? [And here is where it really gets interesting.]

Client: [pause . . . pause . . . pause] I don't know. I guess we could have tried to meet more Black people, but I wouldn't know how.

Me: Maybe this is your opportunity?

Client: I guess I could be open to it. I just never thought about it before.

Aha. Now we're getting somewhere.

That is what makes me excited about this work, and that is what is so aggravating about the state of race in America today. Many of us have "never really thought about it before." We've never been asked to examine our latent beliefs or wonder why we were only exposed to people of our own race in a country that is supposed to be a melting pot.

Of course, the more painful answer to my fourth "Why" above was that my client didn't have any Black people living in her neighborhood because of redlining, which prevented Black families from owning homes in certain neighborhoods and limited their access to financing that would allow them to own property at all. This prevented Black families from building generational wealth. It relegated them to substandard schools in less-desired neighborhoods, locked them out of high-paying jobs, and kept them from intermixing with other races. This was all by design, and it's one of the primary reasons that we still struggle with the racial divide.

For me, being biracial and growing up in a dual-religion household meant that I could live in more than one world at the same time. Now, having a stepmother who is Mexican American and a sister-in-law who is Indian American means that I have the privilege of learning and living with multiple cultures, and I gain access to different worlds because I love people with different identities.

It has always been my perspective that interracial dating affords us the ability to understand one another. Personal experience expands our understanding, and even if someone of another race or culture doesn't end up being your person, your worldview may expand by getting to know them, and theirs by knowing you. What I have discovered in my travels, relationships, and friendships is that we can live by similar values even though our worlds might look very different on the surface. Shared values bond you with someone more quickly than a surface similarity does.

CASE STUDY: THE WHY LEADS TO THE WHO

Geetha came to me ready for marriage. As an Indian American woman over thirty, she faced a lot of pressure from her family to settle down. It's not that she hadn't made the effort but that she'd been dating on the apps for a while and had a few relationships to show for it, but no one had made the final cut. She'd dated men of all backgrounds, but her father made it clear that, for marriage, he would only accept an Indian man. So that was her number one deal breaker when she landed in my office.

I took her through the Five Whys to better understand how she came to this decision and this led us to conclude that her relationship with her family was the most important one in her life. Bringing someone home whom her father would not accept had caused conflict and strife, and her vision for a happy marriage had to have her parents in it. So, we got to work on her dating plan. We hit all the hottest Indian dating apps and within a few weeks she met someone who fit exactly what her dad was looking for. She introduced them and they hit it off, and a few weeks later . . . Geetha and this man broke up. You might think of this as a failure of the dating process, but to me it was a success. She had gotten crystal clear on the match she was looking for and we found that exact person. The system worked. I realized the problem, however, was we weren't matching based on her values and goals but rather those of her parents.

Studies on how we spend our time as we age show that after the age of thirty, time spent with parents decreases significantly; a partner is the only person (other than ourselves) with whom we increase the amount of time we spend as we grow older. This confirms a point that I make often: who you choose to partner with is the most important decision you will ever make in your lifetime—as important as a parent relationship might be, if you match with someone for the happiness of others, you might end up significantly decreasing your own.

ALIGN YOUR VALUES

Values are the engine that drive The Search. If you are clear on your values and those of the person you envision yourself meeting, you will be able to see a path forward. Values tell you where to find this person. Values tell you which app to use. Values tell you how to design your profile to attract the right person.

When we move away from "winning" at the game of love, we step away from quantity and start focusing on qualities. I specifically say *qualities* because a lot of rhetoric in the dating advice field promotes helping people find *quality* matches, yet that point of view assumes that some people have no value. Everyone has value and every person can be a quality match for someone. The key is figuring out who is aligned with you and your unique values.

In my practice, I've seen that values show up in eight major areas. To clarify your values, arrange the following areas of your life in order of priority:

Career fulfillment
Education/personal growth
Family time
Friendships
Health
Financial stability
Philanthropy
Faith

Closely aligned couples generally share two or three top priorities. When you are doing this exercise, there's no good or bad order. However, how you list these priorities often indicates how you allocate your time and energy. Matching with someone who has a similar priority list means you'll usually lead a similar lifestyle and hold a similar vision of how to build your life together. Make sure that those values are reflected in the stories you choose to tell in your profile and what you talk about on your early dates. Not everyone is going to see eye to eye with you. When you pass on a match, it's an opportunity for you to practice empathy.

THANK AND RELEASE

I'm pulling from another feng shui principle when I help my clients navigate this stage of dating by assisting them in releasing what is no longer serving them. One key element of feng shui is to clear clutter—household stuff and mental clutter. They are, in fact, related.

Let's imagine your closet for a second. If you hold onto sweaters that are out of season and pants that are two sizes too small, how do you feel when you go to get dressed? Disappointed? Overwhelmed? Frustrated? But if you release the clutter and emotional weight of the things you don't need, you can actually feel empowered when you are choosing something to wear. You can look at a streamlined closet and see options. Dating operates similarly. If you have a bunch of options in your dating closet that won't fit, culling the field will feel liberating.

In feng shui, before you simply toss out a thing, you acknowledge that there is energy or chi attached to it. You also recognize that at one point this thing had a place in your life but that it no longer does; however, it might hold a place for someone else.

Marie Kondo's method of tidying up uses a similar principle. Examine each thing that is creating clutter, then "thank and release" it. Thanking it honors the role it once held in your life and releasing it cuts the emotional cord and sends it off to find a better home.

I encourage my clients to "thank and release" their matches as well. Whether you find out that they don't share your relationship goals or they stop calling after the third date, it's healthiest to see this as a sign that they were not for you. In your mind, if you *thank and release* them, you can keep on your journey to find the right match without getting stuck in the what-ifs or if-onlys. They were an out-of-season sweater that was too tight and itchy. Though you could probably find a pair of pants to wear with them, they are probably better off out of your dating closet anyway.

Many people you meet will not be dating from a place of empathy, but that doesn't mean you can't still take care of your side of the dating street. Furthermore, honoring their feelings doesn't necessarily mean agreeing with them or giving in to their projections toward you. You cannot control their feelings or actions, but you can control how you respond to them and the feelings that you carry from that interaction.

Taking a moment to internally thank the person whose profile you're passing on and to release them to hopefully find someone else adds humanity back to the dating process. Plus, by releasing them, instead of becoming discouraged or overwhelmed with wrong matches, you're releasing the emotional energy of rejection or of rejecting someone. You're creating space to find your person.

We might follow a certain set of rules for life, and these must be governed by our values. If you have certain beliefs about the way the world works, who you are, and what is important in life, they can guide how you interact with everyone, including dates. I encourage you to write your own rules, though, ones based on your values, rather than trying to live by rules that are based on another person's standards and beliefs.

chapter 7

F the rules,
fix your search

ALTHOUGH THERE ARE STILL "RULES" IN DATING, I WANT YOU to know them not so you can "win" love but so you can chart your own path, one driven by your values and goals. I give you tools instead of rules, so you get to pick and choose the right tools for the right situation. If you understand the fundamentals of what you value and develop a system that puts you in position to meet like-minded people who share those values, this book can take you to a place no rules-based system can go. Having clarity around your values enables you to establish and hold boundaries, which are key in seeing who can meet your dating needs and honor your values.

With your dating mindset sorted, we can move on to devising a strategy that increases your chances of attracting not everyone but the *right kind* of people for you. Unlike the PUA strategy, which teaches tricks that need to be applied in high repetition, this strategy aims to streamline your efforts. PUAs give their clients the confidence to do as many "approaches" as necessary to find a warm lead. It's true that the more you practice dating skills, the easier it is to meet people and the more confident you become, but it's not simply the repetition that makes it work. There has to be an element of understanding and adjustment with each new interaction. You'll be more successful if you're clear on what you're looking for and take a mindful approach to making connections instead of a spray-and-pray method.

A successful dating strategy employs both online and offline methods. Even though you might be frustrated or burned out with dating apps, if you use them in a different way, you can shift your experience. That said, we will begin with the offline methods that are easily accessible to anyone, no matter where you live or what your app expertise might be.

EXERCISE: THE WHERE ARE THEY GAME

How often do you allow yourself to play? We allow children to live in the land of make-believe, but as the challenges of adulthood set in, life becomes far less playful. However, play affects the connections between neurons in the brain's prefrontal cortex, the same part of the brain we covered when clarifying your dating samskaras. These are two skills to master with modern dating because you're constantly having to pick between dating options and keep calm and carry on in the process. I bring a sense of play into the dating search to help my clients stay flexible and navigate the inevitable highs and lows of dating.

Are you familiar with the game Guess Who? Two players each select a mystery person from a deck of twenty-four characters. Each player has a board with all of the characters' faces and the goal is to identify your opponent's character by asking a series of questions: Does your character have facial hair? Is your character wearing glasses? Etcetera. My daughter and I got bored with the traditional style of play, so we took it in a speculative direction and began asking questions about the values and imagined life experiences of our two-dimensional characters.

Questions like "Does your character drive a classic car?" or "Has your character ever traveled abroad?" worked their way into our game play. Even knowing nothing about these two-dimensional characters, the majority of the time one of us can identify the other's character by asking questions about their imagined backstory.

Perhaps this game works because the Guess Who characters have just enough detail in their faces to signify certain undeniable traits and corresponding experiences. Or perhaps it's that my daughter and I share a similar enough vantage point and values system that the pictures mean the same things to us both. Bernard's jaunty hat clearly screams summer stock theater actor to us, but based on your life experiences, you could see deckhand down at the river.

This approach gives us an infinite number of variations on the game, making it more fun to play. More importantly, it also informs my work and helps me give clients playful strategies in dating. Now you get to play with the dating exercise I developed in response; it's called the Where Are They Game.

In the Where Are They Game, you have to use your imagination. There is no way to play this game without guessing, dreaming, and making assumptions about yourself and the person you want to meet.

Building on your work from the Mindset section, take a look at your list of three must-haves. With the three qualities that best describe this person and their values in mind, imagine for a moment where they would spend their time. Where would you meet that person?

> *What are their hobbies?*
>
> *Where do they go on vacation?*
>
> *Where do they eat on their lunch break?*
>
> *Do they go out for a drink after work? Where?*
>
> *Are they involved with any charities?*
>
> *Do they play sports?*
>
> *Do they watch sports? Where?*
>
> *What's their favorite kind of food? Which restaurants would they go to?*
>
> *What kind of music do they listen to? Do they like to hear it live? Where?*
>
> *Which neighborhood do they live in?*
>
> *What do they do for work? Where is their office located?*
>
> *Are they religious? Where do they worship?*

Obviously, you couldn't possibly know exactly where this person lives, what they eat, and how they spend their time, but dreaming up their story can help you figure out where you might meet this person.

Now, looking at this list, we can work backward into designing your "meet cute" moment. Does this guarantee that you will find this specific person in that specific place? Of course not, but it gets you out there into the dating orbit. Setting the stage for how you could cross paths with this person puts you on course to connect with them or at least someone who might share some interests with you. Let's put your answers to the above into action.

If they like to play a sport that you also enjoy, are there any intramural leagues where you might end up playing together?

If they work downtown, which restaurant would they go to during a lunch break? They might be dining solo and eager to find a friend.

If they support a particular charity, could you volunteer to help at its next event?

The purpose of this exercise isn't to make you a Guess Who stalker of your future spouse but to encourage you to put yourself where your match might be. This is something that used to happen organically when we dated in smaller circles. You didn't have to vet your partner for shared values if you knew their mom. You didn't have to make sure you shared the same faith if you met at church. But as our lives have expanded, our matching options have too, and this exercise is an entertaining and effective way to shape your dating circle and improve your chances of meeting someone "the old-fashioned way."

YOUR CONNECTOR'S CIRCLE

Speaking of dating the old-fashioned way, in the before-times, meeting through friends or at a party was the most common way couples connected. Our friends tend to match our values and our friends' friends' values tend to match them as well. Therefore, we can assume that the majority of dates we meet through a friend are prequalified as a values match.

Of course, we might find out further into the relationship that this is not always true, but the endorsement of a friend can earn you a sense of ease and a bit of goodwill on a first date. The dating app Hinge was originally built on this premise. Your matches "hinged" on your Facebook connections and you were matched only with those within a few degrees of social media separation.

We can still re-create that through an exercise I call the Connector's Circle. I find it more effective than simply asking a friend for a setup. If you have ever been set up by a friend, you know you're at the mercy of their Guess Who interpretation of the person you'd match with best. Most friends mean well but tend to set their single friends up with anyone they know who's single; not a great matchmaking strategy. I swung to the other side of this pendulum when my friends never matched me with anyone at all. (I'm still trying not to read into that.)

Your Connector's Circle rests on the same base of your three must-have qualities and one deal breaker. This is your elevator pitch for a match and how you describe what you're looking for. Contrary to popular belief, the language is never "If you know anybody, set me up"—because then you'll just get *anybody*.

Instead, you want to create a network of the people in your world who could know someone who matches your must-haves. Your Connector's Circle usually does not consist of first-degree connections because if they knew someone appropriate, they probably would have already introduced you. But if you can be brave and identify a second level of connections, you'll likely have more luck. Second-level connections might be someone of another generation, someone from work, a neighbor, an acquaintance you do volunteer work with, or someone from church. It's often a person you don't know very well but feel comfortable enough with to share your single status.

Asking for an introduction isn't as awkward as you might think and many clients tell me it's actually easier with second-degree connections because you don't know them as well and are less concerned with the embarrassment. You can simply say, "I'm single right now and looking for someone who is [list your top three must-haves here]:

_____

_____

_____

Let me know if anyone you think I should meet comes to mind." But we can be bold in our search only if we can get over the feeling of single shame.

SINGLE SHAME

Another factor that makes it harder for singles to make connections is the shame around letting it be known that they are looking. Some can't shake the antiquated image of the spinster whose purpose beyond procreation or companionship society struggled to see.

Yet as more women chose to find their purpose in the world or put their careers ahead of their relationship goals, we ended up with a league of superwomen who were confident and successful in many areas of their lives. They were told they could have it all, but, as women leaned into their careers, they leaned out of the dating pool, realizing they could have it all, just not all at the same time.

As that attention got redirected, rather than congratulating women for putting themselves first before moving into a relationship, we kept holding on to our old ideals. Women were simultaneously applauded for getting ahead in life and shunned if they hadn't found a partnership yet. This is when single shame emerged so pervasively.

Folks who hadn't met someone on the timeline that their community deemed appropriate began to see it as a source of embarrassment. Whereas in previous generations a community might have rallied around the single person to support them, as we became more individualized and siloed in our own unique lives and experiences, single people often suffered through their solitude alone. Apps were downloaded in private. Even the utterance that you were single or that you desired a relationship felt unspeakable.

Shani Silver, the host of the *Single Serving Podcast*, shared her thoughts about handling single shame on *Dates & Mates*. Shani said: "I like to remind myself that no one else is living my life. There's no way that my singlehood, the singlehood that belongs to me, could possibly be affecting the people who are shaming me. It's not happening to them. It has zero impact on their life whatsoever, so they have no dog in my fight. I placed that distance between me and the person so their words can have less impact on me."

This is a perfect reminder that others cannot make us feel any particular way. Our emotions are internal, and regardless of the intention of another person, whether it is to help or hurt, we can't prevent them from having their opinion and sometimes voicing it. We only control how we respond to what they've said or done. That feeling of shame is generated internally, often because of our social or familial conditioning. However, if it is coming from inside us, that means that we alone have the power to rewrite that narrative and shift how we let someone else's words or expectations affect us. We cannot get the Connector's Circle to work and lean on our community if we are too embarrassed to tell our community how it can support us.

Women are not the only ones who face these feelings. Here's a question that I received in one of my programs:

> Dear Damona,
>
> Do you have any suggestions on how to deal with the societal pressure to find someone? As a single guy in my mid-twenties, I've felt behind in finding a partner. This feeling is amplified whenever I see my friends enter or maintain long-term relationships and even get engaged or married. I know that this thought is completely false, and that I can develop a satisfying long-term relationship at any age. I just struggle with feeling like I need to achieve this milestone ASAP.

If you relate to this person's situation, I could tell you lots of facts and figures about how you're not behind at all and how it's perfectly normal at any age to feel like you're left out of an exclusive club when you see your peers coupling up. But you won't believe it; not until you have an internal shift. In our society, so much meaning is assigned to partnership, and when so many experiences as well as both legal and social privileges are connected with marriage, I can see why you feel the urgency to "catch up." One thing I know for sure is that this is not a decision you want to rush into or force to happen just because you see everyone else do it. You may feel "behind" because you are taking your time to understand yourself and what you truly want in a relationship. Your timeline is your journey and you have to protect yourself from rushing into a partnership just to keep up with the Joneses.

Although it's important to have relationship role models who show us examples of the kind of love we'd like to have, if spending time with your coupled friends is causing you internal strife, you should try giving yourself a little distance. Similar to how you pay attention to how you feel on a date, you have to consider how you feel with your friends and family too. If every time you get together with someone you're left feeling depressed and self-conscious, you have to consider whether that is the best person or the best situation for you to say yes to. Can you maintain your friendship without always spending time with both people in the couple? Can you spend a little less time with the couples and cultivate new friendships with single buddies who will spend more time in singles' spaces with you? We all know that most couples become boring and lazy about going out after a few months together anyhow.

Fill your time and your emotional cup with the people who bring you joy and raise your vibration so you can attract someone from a place of confidence and fullness. With clarity and patience you will find not just *a* relationship but *the right* relationship for you.

FOMO

As you can see, our drive for partnership doesn't always originate internally. Beyond expectations of friends and family, social media adds another layer of judgment that plays on a 24/7 livestream in our minds. Just as we are finally giving ourselves permission to break from long-held marriage and dating norms, the images on scrubbed-perfect Instagram feeds continually give us the impression that our own lives are lacking.

Pay attention to the messages you consume and remember that social media, much like dating apps, are usually someone's best foot forward. And sometimes those feet are curated, filtered, and faked. Dating with authenticity also means requiring authenticity from those around you and the messages you fill your feed with and consume in real life and online. You have a choice about what you choose to allow in to not just your social feed but also your daily life. If a friend or family member makes you question your worth in singlehood, look at the situation as an opportunity to practice boundary setting and finding your voice. You will need those skills later as you move into dating more seriously.

ONLINE DATING IS JUST DATING

I love giving clients options for meeting dates in person, but the reality is that most of my successful matches have happened on dating apps. What many online daters don't realize, though, is that the two methods aren't as different as we make them out to be. Many of the skills you develop in online dating can be directly applicable to dating "in the wild" and vice versa. When I began as an online dating coach nearly two decades ago, I said,

"Once you get offline and move into the real world, online dating just becomes dating." But thanks to such factors as COVID-19 and the integration of technology into our daily lives, I've simplified that concept to "Online dating is just dating."

A dating app is simply another tool in your dating toolbox. But it's your most powerful tool. Especially as we are constantly looking for ways to shortcut everything, I encourage everyone (even my celebrity clients) to use dating apps to optimize their search.

It's easy to blame dating apps for the downfall of society as we know it. While I understand the frustration many people have with the overwhelming churn of options, with a few tweaks to your online dating experience, you can get the tool working for you.

Beyond simply being a venue for connection, dating apps are also amplifiers. Because the speed of dating increased so dramatically in the last decade, whatever we felt from dating before—be it shame, overwhelm, frustration, fear—it gets amplified because it's now happening at scale. Most singles are having far more dating interactions than they did a decade ago. Even just five years ago, if a client had one date a month, they were ecstatic. Now, clients are sometimes disappointed to have only one date in a week. All of these increased interactions mean there are many more moments in which you will experience the gamut of your feelings, both highs and lows.

Yet there's no denying that dating apps are working for people. Around 40 percent of couples today meet online, and that number has been steadily increasing every year. For LGBTQ and Gen Z daters, that number is even higher.

> *Dear Damona,*
> *I'm a forty-three-year-old woman, never been married and cur-*
> *rently wading the online dating waters. How long do you think is*
> *the "normal" time to keep on trying on the app before admitting*
> *that it's time to pack up?*

Online dating without a plan can feel interminable, but rest assured, there is no set time to discontinue your dating efforts and unplug. This is one reason it's important not to rely on any one method of meeting people. At the point when I cracked the online dating code and was going on multiple dates a week, I actually met more people out and about too. Through online dating, I gained knowledge and confidence by practicing dating skills that I could apply elsewhere. It's simply not a smart dating strategy to completely swear off dating apps entirely because they have critical mass. You have to be where the singles are and the singles are online. Whether it's for practice or to find your forever person, the app is now a vital tool that I encourage clients of all ages to embrace.

FIND YOUR APP MATCH

Choosing the right dating app is almost as important as choosing a match on the app itself. If you dread using your app, feel like there are no options for you, or are confused by the functionality, that's not a reason to walk away from all apps entirely. You might just need a new app or a new approach to get you on your way. Most daters have multiple apps installed on their phone.

Ding. Ding. No, that's not your dating app notifications telling you that you made another match. It's me telling you to focus because you need to understand the differences among apps—and the fact that you might be diluting your efforts being on too many different apps at once.

There are actually four types of dating apps out there. Each comes with its own set of pluses and some minuses that you should be aware of so that you can choose the best app for you right now.

Notice how I said "right now." That's because you are not marrying this app. The goal is for you to get on the app, use it effectively, and then get off of the app and transfer this connection to the real world. You also might find that an app that worked great for you five years ago isn't a good fit right now because you are a dynamic and ever-changing human, just as these apps are constantly being updated too. The popularity of apps changes, the dating pool changes, and your needs change, so stay open to the fact that an app you wrote off a year ago might have your person on it now and an app you used successfully for years might no longer be a good fit for you.

The two factors I encourage my clients to consider when selecting an app are simple:

1. Do you like the pool of people you see when you go through your matches or start swiping?
2. Do you like the functionality of the app?

You have to spend enough time on the app to understand its features and work your way through the dating pool. When most people come to me, they say they've tried dating apps, but when I ask for how long, the average answer is "about a week" or "off and on for years." On average, it takes my clients at least ten *consecutive* weeks to find someone they want to date exclusively. You have to give the app enough time to get its algorithm working for you and to sort your matches.

Here are the four types of apps and the pros and cons of each so you can figure out which is best for your personality type and the time you have to devote to The Search:

Legacy: This is an app that made the transition from desktop dating site to app and is still thriving, such as Match or OkCupid. This type of app has been around for many years and has a large number of people on it. This means you're going to have a lot of options. Yet you're also going to need to do a lot of searching and a lot of screening of matches to find your needle in the haystack. But, hey, it's a pretty big haystack!

Swipe: These are the most popular apps today and include Tinder and Bumble. It's quick and easy to create a profile and start swiping. The plus side: they work fast and they have a lot of users. The challenge: they don't have a ton of information. Whereas legacy apps display all of your likes and hobbies and have different features at your disposal to search for matches, swipe apps prioritize ease of use. This means you can't do an open search. To populate your feed with new people, you must change your preferences, and you can't organize your matches under specific categories.

Curated: This type of app, such as Coffee Meets Bagel or eHarmony, shows you a curated list of vetted options. It shows you a limited number of matches per day. These apps are perfect for you if you tend to get overwhelmed because you don't have to make so many micro-decisions about matches and search methods. If you are having a panic attack after hearing about the legacy and the swipe apps, then a curated app might be for you. But of course there's a catch: you get fewer matches. Curated apps give you a handful of matches per day, so if you want things to change very quickly, these are not necessarily the apps that will create that shift fast. You have to be playing the long game if you're going to do a curated app.

Niche: This is an app with a specific pool, such as Jdate, Christian Mingle, Grindr, or Farmers Only. On the plus side, you know that people you match with on these apps probably meet your core criteria in terms of values, goals, sexual orientation, lifestyle, or another key element of your search. The challenge with the niche apps is that their pools are smaller because everybody is in that particular category already. You're not going to be able to search by as many different factors as you can on a traditional app and you are not going to have as many matches as you would on a swipe app. However, if it is really important that someone meet a specific core criterion, then this is a great option for you.

In September of 2021, I introduced a concept I call "cycling" on *The Drew Barrymore Show*. Cycling is an optimal way to avoid dating burnout because you cycle through a series of two or three apps and you always have new options to look at and new messages coming in.

You start on dating app A for a period of about four to six weeks. If this is an app that you've been on before, you need to make a few changes to your profile to signal to the app that your profile is fresh so it can begin to make new recommendations for you.

Once you hit a lull in activity and feel the momentum slow, you move to app B. Now you're new again, you're boosted in the algorithm, and the dating options start flowing once more. Hit another speed bump? Not to worry, you can go back to app A again or cycle to app C. Here's the kicker, though: during your time on each app, I recommend that you keep only one app on your phone. It's easy to get distracted and overwhelmed if you're on multiple apps at the same time. Time is of the essence on apps. Juggling multiple apps might mean you're missing timely messages and notifications, which could make you miss your dream connection.

ABOUT ME (MEANING, YOU!)

Now on to the bio, the thing that strikes fear into the hearts of men (and women)—writing about oneself. Every dating app has some form of an "About Me" section. It may include writing prompts, but generally, there's an open-ended space where you can write about who you are and what you like. Let the details about yourself shine here. This is not the place to list all of the things that you imagine your perfect partner is or all of the things you hated about your last partner. This is definitely not the place to make demands, which read not only as super List Mythy but also as pretty rude. According to OkCupid, profiles that use phrases like "don't message me if" get fewer matches than those that don't.

Most people dread writing about themselves, but it's actually much easier than you might imagine. Many of the swipe apps have made it even easier by limiting the number of characters you can use in your About Me section and by giving you prompts to help you get started. The most important thing about writing a bio is that you use your limited characters to tell a story, not make a grocery list. You already know what the List Myth will get you. Stories, on the other hand, are memorable, stories draw people in, and stories are unique to you.

If you list all the things you are and all the things you're looking for, then you're probably one of the people who asks me why you never get any better messages than "hey" or, worse, no messages at all because people can't connect with what you wrote or find a unique in to send their first message.

This is a profile list that I've seen variations of hundreds of times: *I'm a kind, smart, and funny woman seeking my partner in crime. I'm looking to meet an honest guy who knows how to treat a lady, loves to travel, and appreciates family.*

When I say storytelling, people often think that means *long*, but it's quite the opposite. A great story is written and then rewritten. It is concise and clear and readers understand the meaning behind the words on the page.

This is a storytelling rewrite of the common list above: *My dad taught me to say hello to strangers and clap at airplane landings. I blush when someone opens my door, cry at romantic movies, and make the best Thanksgiving pumpkin pie.*

These two sets of sentences have the exact same word count, yet the second one exudes the essence of who this person is and includes key details with emotional context that will draw the reader in. The secondary benefit of storytelling is it leaves threads for dates to message you about. The *list sentences* essentially could have been written by anyone, but the *storytelling sentences* include many specifics that could lead into new conversations. A potential date could message about holidays, family time, baking, romantic movies, or their opinion on clapping at airplane landings, which apparently is a very divisive topic, according to news reports.

Some apps make it easy for you by giving profile prompts to answer. Hinge has questions like: "The most spontaneous thing I've ever done . . ." and "I geek out on . . ." Which can lead to passionate, detailed stories in 150 characters or fewer. Challenge yourself to see how clever and descriptive you can be in the least number of characters possible.

On OkCupid, in addition to the classic profile prompts, over five thousand matching questions that you can choose to answer will factor into your profile and matching algorithm in addition to the classic profile prompts: "On a typical Friday night I am . . ." and "Six things I could never do without . . ."*

In the meantime, here are some simple bio writing guidelines to get you going. The kinds of stories that get people to take action by matching and messaging you are the ones that convey the following things:

Nostalgia: Telling a story that includes positive memories from your childhood or adolescence is immediately endearing and can create a feeling of kinship between strangers.

Example: *My mom is still bragging about my sixth-grade violin solo.* This can connect to anyone who played an instrument, likes

---

* If these in-app prompts aren't enough, I offer a Profile Starter Kit with writing prompts and even plug-and-play templates at DamonaHoffman.com.

music, or has had to perform for a crowd, plus anyone who has a mom who likes to brag about them, or wishes they did. Do you have a story that gives a window into who you are, how you grew up, or how you became the person you are today?

Values: Rather than stating your beliefs, talk about a time that reinforced your belief system or gave you an aha moment that confirmed why you believe what you do.

Example: *I went to church to talk to the cute boy down the street. He never spoke to me, but the Lord did.* Christians who are seeking someone who attends church or centers religion in their life might respond to this. Can you think of a story that demonstrates how you live your life and what you believe in?

Humility: Confidence is sexy, but arrogance is off-putting. If you can tell an embarrassing story or allude to the fact that you are in some way humble and self-aware, people will lean in.

Example: *I'll be your best teammate in pub trivia but your worst one in darts.* Can you show your strengths but also be forthcoming about your weaknesses?

Spin that authentic tale of who you are and what makes you tick. Share your hopes, dreams, and hot takes.

Hot Tip: Use passion words and words that evoke feelings. Don't go for the easy word. Go for the word that conveys more meaning and emotion.

Boring words I usually see in profiles: like, enjoy, try, nice, fun, great, cool, sweet, and good.

Passion word examples: love, exciting, explore, motivated, inspiring, fascinating, driven, intrigued, obsessed, curious, insatiable, thrilling, peculiar, unique, intense, wild, courageous, compelling, provocative, delightful, surprising, captivating, unbelievable, incredible, and amazing!

I triple dog dare you to use three or four passion words in a sentence and trade out any of the common words for words infused with more meaning. A thesaurus is a profile writer's best friend.

So, what are you going to write about? Write about activities, interests, goals, experiences, and the things that make you feel alive—anything that you would use passion words to describe.

It's not surprising that the most successful profiles on OkCupid include the word *travel*, *dog*, or *music* because those are things that people speak passionately about. Dog people will never fail to mention their dogs within the first fifteen minutes of a conversation. (I know this because I am a dog person.)

Music bonds people, it evokes a time and place, and it conveys emotion. Use it strategically in your profile. Here's an example: If I say, "I love listening to music," that tells you almost nothing about me. If I say, "I love listening to soul music," that tells you a lot more. But if I say, "Friday nights in my childhood home were filled with Aretha Franklin records and endless games of Spades," you could basically play me in the biopic of my life. The examples you choose can speak to the specific audience you're trying to reach and they'll celebrate the things that are special about you and your life.

Travel is the great unifier. Most people have an interesting travel story to share or an aspirational travel goal to talk about. Painting a picture of a place you'd like to visit with your partner one day brings matches into the conversation and helps them imagine that place as a shared experience.

If you're really stuck or you need a punch-up, I shocked *Dates & Mates* listeners in early 2023 when I declared it was fair game to use an AI text generator to help you find the right words for your profile. The key is that the information you prompt it with must be authentic to you and your story. Then, you should use the AI text as a first draft—never just cut and paste the first result.

People have had friends and experts like my team and me assist them with crafting their story in dating profiles for years. Now we have even more tools at our disposal to level the playing field and improve our written communication. As long as the information is authentic and specific to you, I don't see it as misleading to use these tools to put your best foot forward. Some of them also level the playing field for daters with disabilities who may otherwise struggle with the written elements that are unavoidable in online dating. New technology often creates fear and confusion, but I always look for ways to use it to enhance our lives and free up ourselves from frustrating tasks so we can conserve our energy for more important things, like connecting face-to-face with other humans.

A PICTURE SPEAKS A THOUSAND WORDS

Less is more when it comes to profile photos. People often confuse their dating app with their Instagram feed. We're not going for likes, we're going for substance. And filters are definitely out when it comes to dating apps. Some apps even eliminate photos that are heavily filtered. AI generators are off limits when it comes to pictures because they alter your image in ways that might set your date up for feeling misled. Think of your profile as a curated selection of pictures that tell the (authentic) story that you want to tell to potential dates.

Let me explain most daters' thought process when swiping:

Photo 1: Interesting, cute.
Photo 2: Different look, nice.
Photo 3: Oh, what's that about?
Photo 4: Ew, I don't like that shirt.
Photo 5: Pass.

Daters go from interest to repulsion in the span of five or six photos. Your profile is only as good as your worst photo, and the order in which you display them matters.

I created a rubric to help clients remember the three must-haves for their curated profile photo collection: the Three Cs: color, context, and character.

Color: If you use a bold color in your primary photo, you'll stand out from the crowd. From a strategic point of view, red is the color that is most likely to draw someone's eye to you. Think about how red shows up in your life. You instinctually notice red stop signs. Red lights. Red flags. Well, maybe you don't see red flags and that's why you're reading this book. Either way, you might be interested to know that red commonly shows up for other animals as a sign of arousal. Does the color have the same effect on us?

A 2008 study at the University of Rochester examined how men responded to various colors. Researchers showed the male participants photos of a number of women. Some pictures had red borders and others had different colored borders. Then, the men were asked to rate the women's attractiveness. The women with the red borders consistently were ranked as more attractive than the women with the green borders. Yet what many of the men may not have realized is these were pictures of the same women, just with different colored borders around their images. Red doesn't seem to have the same effect on women, so if you're a cishet guy, don't run out and buy an entire wardrobe in red. Also, I should add that same-sex attraction was not included in this study. However, I find that a bold, bright color—either in clothing or in the background of a picture—is a winning strategy for all genders and orientations, particularly in your primary photo, to stand out from the crowd. The little black dress is so 2019. It's not a hard-and-fast rule, but color is a tool you can use to stand out.

If you don't have colorful clothing, search for popular murals or Instagram-friendly backdrops in your area. An estimated one hundred thousand people take snaps at the "selfie wall," a bubble-gum pink monolith that costs the Paul Smith store in Los Angeles $60,000 a year to maintain. Because of the amount of traffic the famous store parking lot receives, it is officially designated as a city landmark. In 2009, I bought a suit for my husband at this store. Back then, parking was easy and I didn't have to fight through throngs of tourists to get to the front door. The store had the same signature pink wall then, but there was one major difference: Instagram had not yet been invented. As soon as a few Instagrammers revealed the magic visual, we mere commoners hoped our photos would pop against that bright pink backdrop too. Influencers have the Three Cs down because they are masters of attracting attention. That is exactly how you should be thinking for your profile photos. Your dating profile is marketing. Your pictures are the billboard advertising you to your suitors—they are the wink from across the bar, the hankie being dropped, the calling card left behind of the modern era of dating.

Context: A picture speaks a thousand words. So, rather than lamenting the fact that no one reads anymore or looking at it as a sign that they're just not that into you because they didn't review your bio with highlighter in hand, consider the benefits of a visual medium. You can actually gain back some real estate in your dating profile by infusing context into your photos. If you love to hike, show a picture of yourself on the trails; bonus points for an interesting background with a story behind it (hello, Grand Canyon).

Let's say you don't really hike but you aspire to one day hike and you've been thinking a lot about the lifestyle of hiking. Let's say you like the idea of attracting someone who hikes. Let's say you used to hike ten years ago but you blew out your knee and can't really huff it uphill anymore. Do not use a photo of yourself hiking.

Honesty is still the most important element in your profile. If you don't have any current hobbies, and you haven't traveled anywhere, you don't play any games, you're not interested in sports, and you haven't read any interesting books lately, then I'm not sure dating is the problem. Find something that you're passionate about and that will help you find someone who is passionate about you.

Character: This is the profile element that most people overlook. We have been conditioned to chase likes. We are told to lock away our goofy, nerdy, quirky, humorous, irreverent, bookish, intense, or sensitive sides so we don't turn someone off, so we aren't "too much." You can only stuff away those parts of yourself for so long before they pop back up. I've seen far too many relationships end because both parties were on best behavior while they were dating, in order to be likable, then became someone else after cohabitation or marriage.

There is a measurable benefit to being more specific in your profile. In the book *Dataclysm*, OkCupid cofounder Christian Rudder proved that it's better to be polarizing than to fall in the middle of the road. OkCupid used to allow daters to rank their matches on a 5-point scale, 5 being "hubba-hubba," 1 being "ew, gross." Rudder found that being highly polarizing, meaning some people considered you a 5 while others considered you a 1, got you 70 percent more messages than if you tended to be consistently ranked in the middle of the road.

Rudder interpreted this to mean that if a man viewed a woman as conventionally attractive, he might assume he was in competition with a lot of other suitors and move on. I believe this is part of it, but I think this data also points to the popularity-by-polarization trend that we are all keenly aware of today.

Look no further than our current political landscape to see how being loathed by some results in being loved even more by others. If a match sees you as a kindred spirit, they are more likely to make a connection and more motivated to keep the conversation going because they have more to go on than just a pretty face—they have common ground to build a relationship from. Beauty may fade, but a true connection has legs, perhaps of both the literal and metaphorical sort.

Now that you know the various elements, let's put it all together because a search without the foundation is just a waste of time. Time is our most valuable nonrenewable resource, so we have to be deliberate about how we use it. Having a dating app installed on your phone is not the same thing as *dating* on a dating app. You could be doing a lot of dating busywork that makes you feel like you're putting yourself out there but really all that effort has earned you is anxiety and disappointment.

THE TEXTING TRAP

Let's say you've run the gauntlet and you matched with someone you actually like. Getting to the date requires you to clear one more hurdle—the Texting Trap. Though I still believe that texting is largely for information, not conversation, culture has shifted and I'm not one to stand in the way of the wheels of progress. About ten years ago, I noticed in my practice that people were coming to me for guidance on texting. They were confused about how to respond to potential dates, they wanted to know how to create intimacy through emojis, and they wondered why people they really liked weren't texting them back.

I realized that I needed to support my clients through this emerging phase of dating. This wasn't a distraction in the dating process. Suddenly, texting had become an official step in assessing who was a match for you and a vital skill for my clients to develop . . . and fast.

The perils of texting were still apparent to me, however. I watched in real time as otherwise strong bonds were broken through interrupted texting cadence or misunderstandings about what was being said. I witnessed clients falling for false narratives behind those little colorful text bubbles. I saw the communication backslide unfolding, and I was powerless to stop all of culture from texting. I couldn't stop it, but I could name it . . . the Texting Trap.

The first time I offered a Texting Trap webinar in 2015, the virtual room was packed. Over five hundred people clamored to understand why texting was creating so much confusion for them and how to escape from a dead text thread fate. I call it a trap because, no matter how comfortable we all become with texting, it will never be a substitute for synchronous communication or in-person connection. There is always room for misinterpretation. There is always the invisible specter of doubt that creeps in when you see those dreaded three dots appear and disappear. Are they going to respond or not? We become paralyzed in the trap.

Even so, you can improve at texting. You can get better at expressing yourself clearly and authentically. You can be schooled on the ever-changing texting cultural norms (which hopefully are not already obsolete by the time you're reading this book). You can become more skilled at reading between the lines to improve your text interpretation skills.

The great thing about studying the Texting Trap is that this skill is completely transferrable, and once you learn how to text your dates better, you'll also notice your text banter improving with friends and loved ones.

THE TEXTING TEN COMMANDMENTS

I followed up the Texting Trap training with another class called "The Texting Ten Commandments," which helped my clients understand not only the challenges of texting but also the principles to navigate through them. Much like the Ten

Commandments are a guideline for living a virtuous life, here are the Texting Ten Commandments so you can have a virtuous cycle of texting:

1. THOU SHALT AVOID GENERIC QUESTIONS. Go beyond good morning and ask thoughtful questions that inspire a reply.
2. THOU SHALT NOT OVERWRITE. More than three sentences in a single message will usually be skimmed or overlooked. Focus on what is most important for you to say.
3. THOU SHALT NOT MISUSE EMOJIS. If you're nervous about using an emoji out of context, just pick your classic three or four signature emojis that best express you—and in most cases use only one emoji at a time.
4. THOU SHALT USE MULTIMEDIA. Use more than just the written word to convey your intention: GIFs, memes, and links can transform your text connection.
5. THOU SHALT KNOW WHEN TO WALK AWAY. Don't double-text to force a reply.
6. THOU SHALT SHOW THY PERSONALITY. Write like you speak and be yourself over text. Don't cut and paste the same messages to multiple people to hedge your bets, as it will come off as generic.
7. THOU SHALT NOT FIGHT OR ANTAGONIZE. It's hard enough to understand tone over text, so texting is not the best venue to win an argument.
8. THOU SHALT NOT SEND A DRUNK TEXT. Just don't. This is one of my few universal dating rules.

9. THOU SHALT NOT X-RATED SEXT. The cloud never for-
   gets, and even though revenge porn is illegal, it still
   happens.

10. THOU SHALT NOT ABUSE THE QUEEN'S ENGLISH. Dat-
    ing app users say they will unmatch someone for
    spelling errors—just make sure you're autocorrect is
    working for you. I mean *your* autocorrect. See, it
    can happen to anyone.

Use the Texting Ten Commandments as tools and not rules.
It's most important to text authentically and break the robotic
texting cycle so many of us got stuck in.

TIMING

The first thing you have to understand about texting is timing is
everything. The average response time to a text is roughly ninety
seconds. You are competing for your date's attention against
everything else in their phone, so you can't take too long to
respond, but of course you can't be too eager either.

Texts usually happen in short bursts of communication called
"text threads." A thread could be as short as a few minutes or as
long as a couple of hours. Think of a text thread as a short conversation that takes place in writing. It's kind of like the olden
days, when suitors would leave their calling card and letters
would be exchanged before the courtship phase began in earnest,
but on speed.

To feel out your text timing, you must develop a sense of
when the text thread is complete and when it's time to let the

conversation rest. Usually, this is signaled by your date dropping hints that they need to go or taking longer and longer to respond to your messages. People often think that keeping their date texting longer will lead to a higher chance of it working out, but the opposite is actually true. If you overshare over text or keep them texting longer than they'd like, they'll feel depleted and less excited about moving your conversation to the next level.

Aim to respond to DMs (direct messages), messages in a dating app, or texts with new matches within twenty-four hours. At this point, the other person has no emotional investment in you and it's easy to move on to the next match if they feel you're unresponsive or interpret your slower messages to mean lack of interest.

From there, I recommend daters hold off on texting too much until you've hit the magical three-date milestone and you graduate into the next phase, when you're actually dating in the real world and not just becoming texting pen pals.

> Dear Damona,
> I follow your advice on Dates & Mates but I don't know what to say to stop matches from texting before dates. Is there a way to let them know I'm interested but I want to save it for the date?

In the early phase of texting, especially prior to the first date, it's important to generate enthusiasm but also set boundaries in a respectful way. When a client feels the gravitational pull of the

Texting Trap starting to drag them down as their date starts asking personal questions and sending daily check-in texts before they've even met, I suggest they respond with something like: "I would love to tell you more about that in person. Looking forward to Friday!" Don't overexplain any boundary you give. Simply make the statement, express enthusiasm, and then let it lie until time to confirm or go on the date.

And always confirm the date. With many text or app message threads happening simultaneously, it's not uncommon for someone (or for you) to drop the ball on a date you're actually excited about. Try not to take it personally, but also try to reconfirm your dates eighteen to twenty-four hours in advance with an enthusiastic message to make sure you're not sitting at home all dressed up with nowhere to go the next day.

ESCALATION

The date expectation starts building from the minute you and your date match and start texting. Instead of thinking of the text as a way to vet your date, think of it as your opportunity to expand your curiosity and amplify the chemistry for the first few dates.

You can do this by asking light questions that give you a sense of their personality. If you met online, lead with the thing in their profile that you're most intrigued to learn more about. Also, look for possible common ground for date ideas within their profile and in this texting phase. Find out what they do for fun to give you insight into the kind of dates you could do together to step away from the traditional dinner or drinks. Get a sense of the kind of music they listen to for insight into the venues or bars they'd be most comfortable at. Look for just enough common ground, witty banter, and enthusiasm to suggest an in-person date.

PERSONAL TOPICS

My client Gina had a potential date ask over text why she and her ex divorced. Assuming that it would be rude to ignore the question, she gave this man the truth: her ex-husband cheated on her. Once she was done baring her soul to this stranger over text, she felt overexposed and, worse yet, they never ended up going out.

Just as when you're on the date, I believe your date needs to earn information. You can't just give them the whole story up front. They have to demonstrate that they care about your stories and you can trust them enough to share your soul.

What if you get a question that you don't want to answer? Try one of my coy redirection responses or create your own:

I'd love to tell you more about that when we meet.
I'll never kiss and tell.
Once we have a few martinis/glasses of wine/beers, maybe
   I'll share that story.
Funny story but it's better told in person.

We want to save as much information as possible to be revealed on the date. You have to build anticipation from date to date and leave more to be discovered.

EMOJI MAGIC

Before you turn your nose up and tell me that emojis are for twelve-year-old girls, hear me out. They are actually a very efficient way of conveying information and can be used in place of punctuation for a more effective message.

First, emojis are mood modifiers. This means that by adding them to the end of a thought or sentence, you actually change the meaning and convey tone.

A phrase like: *When are we going out?* can be read as curt standing alone. But add an emoji like: *When are we going out* 😉 and now it's flirtatious.

Emojis work particularly well to indicate your sense of humor. If you are being sarcastic, you can follow up a statement with a 😂😄 or at the very least a 🙂 to make sure the tone comes across.

Second, emojis show that you don't take yourself too seriously and you will have fun on a date. Emojis are like salt, though. A little bit enhances the flavor of what you're writing, but too much and it's overpowering.

READ IT ALOUD

We process information differently when we hear a voice. The speech signals in our brains turn on and we can catch tonal shifts and errors more easily. If you're not sure how a message sounds, take a moment to read it aloud before you send. Then try to read it with a different emotion behind it to see if the message could be misinterpreted. Could you sound peeved saying the same words? Could you read it with a negative attitude? Could you be angry? Does it potentially sound like you're talking down to the recipient or being critical?

If you're still not sure whether you should send a message, appoint a text buddy, someone you send your texts to who can give you feedback in a timely manner before you send them to dates.

THE CALLBACK TECHNIQUE

Old texting rules said to never double-text, meaning don't send a follow-up text if someone doesn't respond to you. Though this is still a good idea, nowadays it's preferred that we break up large chunks of text into two or three shorter statements. Still, with so many messages flooding into our phones, sometimes folks just get lost in the shuffle.

One of the most effective tools for building a rapport with someone over text is the "callback technique" in which you call back something that you discussed previously, either in the thread or on prior dates. This is also an excellent way of reinvigorating a text thread that has gone silent.

Let's say a match mentions a particular restaurant that they love. Send them a picture of the restaurant as you're driving by, with a note like "This made me think of you" or "Now I'm craving burgers" or, even more direct, "We should grab a bite here next week!" If they are interested, they will take the bait and restart the thread.

Callbacks work especially well with references to things that could lead to specific dates, such as musical interests, games, sports, and other activities. References to famous people are also great for callbacks because you're likely to come across an article, tweet, or bit of gossip that you can text them with a simple "Did you hear this?"

When you are using a callback, it's best not to set it up too overtly. You are referencing a moment or a detail you shared, so the connection should be obvious. If you have to remind the person first that you discussed the topic, the idea is probably not right for a callback.

My favorite style of callback is a little bit of text paired with a GIF or meme because then usually humor is implied. If you can make your date laugh or smile, you can trigger their dopamine, serotonin, and endorphins to release, which will make them associate positive feelings with you and feel eager to connect with you again for another hit of neurochemicals. Plus, doesn't it make you feel good to make someone else laugh and smile?

Are there rules in dating? There are, but dating rules are not a one-size-fits-all approach. You write the rules for your own dating life. We have spent far too long trying to jam our toes into Cinderella's slipper when there is a slipper for every foot. To find that slipper, you don't need to manipulate it and you don't need to make it feel like less of a shoe. You also don't need to compete with tons of other shoppers in a race to get a single slipper on your foot. This isn't a Black Friday sale. There are enough matching pairs to go around.

This method of dating is deliberate and it does take time and focus, but the results are far better and the process more fulfilling. I'd propose that this is part of the reason that, over the last few decades, divorce rates have reversed the upswing they were on previously. New couples are being more thoughtful about who they choose to partner with and are understanding the importance of having a shared outlook on the world through similar values.

Conversely, among the fifty-plus age demographic, divorces are actually increasing rapidly. Women who believed the fairy tale or weren't given the freedom of mate choice are waking up to see that they hold the keys to their destiny now. Men are realizing that they need more than a pretty face to make it last long term. And LGBTQ+ singles now have the option to marry the person who is meant for them. This is all happening while younger daters, who grew up with social media and dating apps, know that their ideal person might not be in their immediate social circle or geographic area but see connection opportunities using the technology they are so familiar with. No one wants to settle for a loveless, uninteresting partnership, and thankfully now, no one has to. If you are willing to commit to self-discovery and use that knowledge to be mindful about your search for love, you can have it all.

THE SEARCH ACTION STEPS

1. *Order your values.* Take the time to truly identify your values and how you wish to live your life with your future person.
2. *Find your tribe.* Using a combination of imagination and networking, figure out how to expand your social circle to include someone who could be a match.
3. *Match with an app.* Embrace dating apps as the most powerful tool in your dating toolbox and identify the best app to focus on.
4. *Escape the Texting Trap.* Create enthusiasm for your in-person dates by encouraging real, honest communication.

part III

the date

the chemistry myth

ONCE UPON A TIME, THERE WAS A PRINCE WHO ALWAYS HAD A dance for the ball, but as soon as the clock struck midnight, it seemed that all the magic and romance would fade away. The prince was desperate to feel something, anything, so he kept going to balls and dancing in circles, but in the end, it just left him dizzy and tired. Soon he realized it wasn't about the number of dances he did, it was about being focused on the dance he was doing at that very moment.

At this point, you might have a clear head about dating and a process to find your people, but then you go on a date and it feels like you're in the movie *Groundhog Day*. You're running the same script with everyone you meet, and if you have to repeat your life story or explain your job one more time, you swear you're going to delete the dating apps permanently (again). You just want to feel something. If only a spark of chemistry could shake you out of your routine. I know what you're wishing for because I've been there myself.

CATCHING CHEMISTRY

The minute I saw his profile, I felt that indescribable thing: the yearning, the connection, the anticipation. As an online dating newbie, he was nervous about meeting up, and as a digital dating veteran by that point, I calmed his fears and we locked in plans for the following evening. I arrived carrying curiosity but also a strange sense of confidence because this connection seemed sure in a way I hadn't felt for some time.

He walked through the doorway at Lola's and I sized him up. Yes, that was definitely him and, yes, the feeling was definitely still there. I waved him over, he gave me a hug to say hello, and in that moment I knew. That fire sizzling inside me was a familiar feeling. I'd felt it with that kid in high school from the football team. I'd felt it with that guy I worked with at the movie theater. It was there with that creative collaborator in college. I'd felt it for that friend of a friend everyone said was bad news (he was), the man from Burning Man, the translator, the musician, the editor, the actor (well, a lot of the actors). Now here again, I felt it—instant chemistry.

Three hours and three martinis later, in my mind we were already married. He was so enthralled with our conversation that he called his brother to tell him my favorite musical. Somehow, his brother didn't share our enthusiasm about Sondheim's underrated classic *Company* at his midnight, our 10:00 p.m. The sparks were so strong, along with the martinis, that I thought nothing could alter this feeling. He was heading back to his hometown for a few days, but he told me we'd have another date next week.

As I waited for that call, I told all my friends about him. Surely, they were going to love him and, surely, me being patient for a few days was nothing compared to our lifetime ahead. But a week went by and no word. After another week, nothing. I knew what was happening but still sought closure, so I put everything I had to say in an email and hit send. Eventually, I did get a reply. When he was on his trip, he'd gotten back together with his ex-girlfriend. Our chemistry did not conquer all.

THE CHEMISTRY MYTH

My story is not unusual. The Chemistry Myth has a hold on many of my clients and listeners. Romantic comedies and romance novels have told us that we should feel butterflies when we meet our person. We chase butterflies because we don't actually understand what they mean.

That buzzy feeling is not just in your mind, either. Butterflies are the feeling you get when adrenaline sends blood away from your stomach to other muscles, preparing you to spring into action. That nervousness is your sympathetic nervous system kicking in with your fight-or-flight response. On a physiological level, chemistry is getting your body ready for what comes next.

In the animal kingdom, I can see why one might need to pounce on a mate at first glance because who knows when the next viable option might scurry through the forest. In our society, though, so much more goes into mate selection.

In 2021, I interviewed dating coach Logan Ury on the NPR podcast *Life Kit* about her book *How to Not Die Alone*. Her client case studies drove her to the same conclusion about chemistry, which she turned into a chapter of her book: "F**k the Spark." We both have seen that when clients chase this feeling, it usually ends in disappointment or heartbreak.

Although many people hold out hope that they'll know it when they see it or they'll feel the spark instantly when they meet "The One," it's actually quite liberating to release the notion that if we don't feel butterflies immediately, it's not meant to be. You can't be too quick to dismiss chemistry as a lie, just like you can't take it at face value and assume it's telling the truth. You must take it in as a data point, one of many that you are collecting in the dating process.

We lean in to the Chemistry Myth because it's easier to believe than to put in the time to develop a relationship. It retains our sense of magic in the process of finding love. If love is just a game of chance, then you get to skip the hard stuff. You can avoid the awkward introspection. You can fast-forward through the frustrating first dates. You can give yourself an easy exit away from feelings of rejection if you can just chalk the differences up to a lack of chemistry. If we can dismiss someone based on butterflies alone, we don't have to explain. The pursuit of chemistry keeps us from digging deep to explain our values or opening up and letting someone in. But the pursuit of chemistry also means letting good matches slip through our fingers because we were not patient enough to see what lies beyond our first impression.

AT FIRST GLANCE

Examining the root of those first impressions can lead us to some interesting places. When we feel that burst of adrenaline, what is our sympathetic nervous system responding to? The simple answer is that it's usually driven by our instinct to seek similarity. We seek out familiarity or perceived similarity because we assume we'll have more in common and the road to a relationship will be less rocky.

That adrenaline kicks up as we assess who this person before us is. Are they safe? Or do we need to flee? Rarely do we read butterflies as a sign of impending disaster; instead, we lean in, intrigued.

Dr. Drew Pinsky summed it up best in my four-hundredth episode of *Dates & Mates* when he suggested that we ask whether we are feeling butterflies or lightning bolts. Moderate attraction, which is often accompanied by that fluttery sensation, can sometimes grow, but intense attraction, the kind that leaves you tongue-tied and weak in the knees, is usually a signal from your body. Dr. Drew went on to say, "The body is a perfect instrument," meaning you should pay attention to the signals your whole body is sending you. We tend to have selective body listening, especially when we are on a date.

We don't start by listening with our whole body; most people begin with the eyes. Our first impression is largely based on the way someone looks. In 2020, 90 percent of respondents in the Match app's annual Singles in America study said that physical attractiveness was important to them in a long-term partner.

And now we're being programmed to distort our image into a singular ideal by photo-editing software and social media filters. Facetune, one of the original photo-editing apps, has preset filters that claim to enhance your features. Enhancement includes removing blemishes, freckles, and wrinkles; changing your skin tone; and even altering the shape or color of your eyes. Moreover, as we become accustomed to viewing Facetuned photos, we are losing our grip on what real faces and unaltered versions of attractiveness look like.

The eye editing feature is significant because of our nature as visual creatures. Predators evolved to have eyes that face forward to pursue their prey. We're the most successful predators on the planet, with undeniable front-facing eyes to prove it. A prey animal, like a horse, chicken, or deer, has side-facing eyes to take advantage of their peripheral vision. These animals often rely on their other senses to paint a full picture of what's happening and where danger may be coming from. Not us. We are forward-looking, other-sense-ignoring creatures. I believe this is one of the reasons we are so influenced by the eyes in dating. If we can't see someone's eyes clearly, we question whether we can trust them.

Fun fact: According to Tinder, OkCupid, Zoosk, and Hinge, your likability drops if you're wearing sunglasses in your dating profile photo. We all think we look cooler in sunglasses, but by making us appear mysterious and intriguing, sunglasses make it harder for potential matches to read intent, take facial cues, and connect from a more vulnerable place.

Humans love a big eye. Mascara owes a large chunk of its market share to this preference. A Google search for "how to make your eyes look bigger" returns pages of articles and tutorials on how to create a smokey eye and make our peepers pop.

There's science behind our attraction to the big eye. A 2015 study from Leiden University in the Netherlands set up participants to play trust games with computer-generated partners. The eyes of the partners were modified to appear either large with pupils dilated or static with pupils constricted. Researchers found that people were more likely to trust the partners whose eyes were large and dilated. Participants' eyes were recorded dilating in response to those partners, as well.

BEAUTY IS IN THE EYE OF THE BEHOLDER

To get beyond the Chemistry Myth, we have to acknowledge how much we are influenced by our environment and biological conditioning. Washboard abs serve little purpose in modern life unless you are a global Iron Man competition junkie (but if you are, definitely use those photos in your dating profile). Yet we are predisposed to pay attention to washboard abs because of what they signify: strength, capability, health, and the media reinforces our ab ideals.

However, the media we consume matters. Renaissance paintings promoted curvy bodies as the peak of health four centuries ago. That look was hard to attain at that time if you lived modestly and barely had enough to eat. Plus, back then, Brazilian butt lifts (a.k.a. BBLs) were a thing of fiction. Beauty standards are so situational, so regional, so generational, and so ephemeral.

The standard of beauty differs depending on the population you're dating within. I noticed this acutely when I moved from a predominantly white suburb of Chicago to the melting pot city of Los Angeles. I didn't have to press my curls straight to be seen as beautiful. No one asked if they could touch them, like I was a prize pony, because hair like mine was just part of the norm. Still, a priority is placed on Anglo beauty standards in many parts of the world. Blepharoplasty, a cosmetic eyelid adjustment, not only is popular among Asian Americans but also is the most popular surgery in Asia. Globally, we are chasing the same standard of beauty, even if it's not our natural look.

Yet in some places, the very features or qualities we've learned to see as deficits are the very things that make us attractive. In 2015, I wrote an article for BET.com about the experiences of Black women dating outside of the United States. Many of them reported feeling overlooked and underappreciated dating in America, but abroad they were revered for their beauty.

We've established that humans find comfort in familiar faces. If you're a tabloid reader, look no further than the rotating cast of who's dating who in Hollywood. Many stars seem to pick carbon copies of their exes. To say Leonardo DiCaprio has a thing for young blondes is an understatement. Each person we fall for leaves their imprint on us in many ways. Even if the relationship didn't end well, if you were once attracted to something about them, you may subconsciously be drawn to similarities in future matches.

What happens when we get curious about our attractions? When we understand where our patterns come from, we are no longer subject to the whims of our initial instinct and we can actually lay a foundation for the future.

Everything you truly want in a relationship lies beyond chemistry and instant attraction. You've probably experienced what happens when the sparks wear off and you're left with the charred embers of an incompatible relationship. The more you got to know one another, the less you had in common, and perhaps you wondered what would be different if you'd had deeper conversations earlier on.

To sustain a relationship long term, you need to be able to truly communicate with one another. This means there are going to be some speed bumps along the way and how you navigate them together is what will truly set the right match for you apart from the rest.

According to OkCupid data, we are trending in the right direction. Over half of the daters surveyed said that they are open to dating someone who is not their traditional type. In person, you can be intrigued by many aspects of someone's personality, but we still rely heavily on our traditional type for that first swipe.

OPERATION DNG

When my boss originally suggested I try online dating, it wasn't because I wasn't meeting anyone. It's because she thought I wasn't meeting the right type of guys. And she was right. I was addicted to the emotional roller coaster. I was addicted to unpredictability and leaned in to any dating experience that kept me guessing. She knew there were nice guys out there who would treat me with respect, so she insisted that I try dating her way: online.

Yet pulling up a chair at the great dating buffet can be overwhelming without clarity and intention, so we gave ourselves a mission in this new way of dating. We called it Operation Date

Nice Guys (or Operation DNG, when we were speaking in code at the office). Of course it was corny; of course it seemed ridiculous to strategize our dating plans like we were CIA operatives on a love mission, but today I'm so grateful for Operation DNG because it worked.

The minute he walked in the door at Lola's (yes, it was always Lola's) for our first date, I sized him up: a black sweater neatly arranged on top of a green button-down shirt, gray wool pants, sensible shoes, and a haircut that screamed reliable. He literally looked like he'd walked out of a Banana Republic. This was not my type, I immediately thought. Where is his motorcycle, where is his hair gel, can we at least get a leather jacket? He looked so . . . so . . . so . . . nice. But he was so cute, so I thought maybe I could set him up with someone else.

This dialogue all happened in my brain within the first seven seconds of meeting him. "Wait, the mission," I thought. "What about Operation DNG?" I was supposed to be dating nice guys. I snapped out of it and reminded myself that my "type" was my old programming and I recommitted to the mission at hand. I reassured myself that dating against type was going to look and feel different, and that brought me back to the present moment.

Being with this nice guy was 180 degrees from what my dating experience was before. He was thoughtful and kind. He made me feel seen. He made me feel safe. I had to break my pattern of falling into chemistry because it was signifying the wrong things. Those butterflies were red alert signals and I was reading them as green lights. I had been in survival mode in dating for so long, I didn't know what safety felt like. Operation DNG saved me.

the communication pillar

E FFECTIVE COMMUNICATION LEADS TO A MORE ENJOYABLE dating experience. Trade chemistry for curiosity and your dates will never be dull. When you're no longer longing to feel a spark, you can focus on discovery. What are you learning about the other person in the time you have together? What are you learning about yourself?

The flip side of chasing chemistry and expecting to feel something the first time you meet is taking the time to communicate effectively in the early days of a relationship. It's not about avoiding all conflicts and keeping a relationship on the sizzling surface. There's crucial discovery in seeing how someone solves a problem and what happens when they are under pressure or clarifying a phrase they said that you misinterpreted. There's magic in having compelling conversations that make you lean in to their words before you've even jumped into bed together. The next pillar is developing clear communication.

You're responsible for your own good time, so if you don't like a topic of conversation, you need the confidence and skill to shift the direction. You don't need an outgoing, bubbly personality to ace your dates. Connection comes from being a clear and engaging communicator, which is not the same as being the loudest person in the room. Often, introverts can be better daters because, even though people might tell you that they want to date someone extroverted, they are more likely to give a second date to someone who listens well than to someone who overtalks the whole time.

For years, I would send my clients out on mock dates with one of my team members whose sole job was to go on pretend dates and review my clients based on a list of date success skills (pretty cool gig, if I do say so myself). One of the key questions on the evaluation form was who did more of the talking? An A+ client would have the mock dater report that they both talked about evenly. But, of course, that rarely happened. Prior to the mock dates, I would instruct my client to focus on listening and aim for a 70/30 listening-to-talking ratio, which would probably net out at 50/50. Still every time, my mock dater would report feeling like the client was speaking the majority of the time.

This is what happens when nerves kick in. We start thinking about how we can impress the other person and we get to tap dancing. We think the more we talk, the more interesting we become, but studies on communication say the exact opposite.

According to research from Harvard published in the *Journal of Personality and Social Psychology*, people who asked more questions during a conversation, specifically follow-up questions, were perceived as more likable.

When you focus more on listening, you can stay in the moment rather than letting chemistry catapult you into the future or your mind anchor you to the past. Listening with curiosity inspires you to ask great questions that clarify the stories your date is telling you and reveal more about who they are and whether or not they're a good match for you.

Remember that when we feel chemistry, it is usually a signal from our brain that it's being hijacked by adrenaline. This is the same neurochemical that stimulates our fight-or-flight response, but there is one other response animals have in high-stress situations. It's not only fight or flight. It's actually fight, flight, or freeze. Have you ever seen an actual deer in headlights? We use that phrase as an analogy for when someone is unsure of what to do next because deer often freeze in the face of danger. So do daters.

In a segment on *The Drew Barrymore Show*, I did a dating red flags quiz with Alicia Silverstone and Drew. I posed the question: Is it a red flag when your date doesn't ask any questions about you? Drew and Alicia both raised their red flags emphatically, but I had to offer a counterpoint. There are situations when someone not asking *follow-up questions* is a red flag. Especially if the lack of questions is coupled with a judgmental remark, a rude comment to the waiter, or any action that makes you feel uncomfortable or doesn't honor what you're feeling. However, there are times when someone's nervous system is so overwhelmed on a date that they get stuck in freeze mode.

Most people hate first dates and don't feel like they can truly be themselves when they first meet someone. Usually, this stems from lack of practice, but sometimes a person is just so taken by chemistry that they can't connect with the person in front of them. We read lack of questions as lack of interest or arrogance when sometimes it's actually the opposite. What can be interpreted as disinterest can actually be an overwhelmed sympathetic nervous system trying to freeze its way out of an awkward encounter. It's challenging to overcome a nervous-system takeover in the moment. Anyone in the armed forces will tell you that the best way to stay calm in a high-stakes situation is by preparing in advance.

To prepare for the inevitable uncertainty of a first date, we must rewind the clock to the time before the date begins. First, I have my clients reread their date's profile and make a "curiosity list" before the date. This is a list of anything intriguing they'd like to learn more about. Next, I take them through flirting classes to get them comfortable in their own skin and improve their communication skills. If you've never role-played a challenging conversation or written down talking points to make sure you mention what's most important, you haven't really lived!

Dear Damona,

I'm trying really hard on dating apps to look for the right kind of people who have the same values as me who want commitment. I go on these dates, and then I just have no chemistry with these guys at all. Yet, when I bump into a guy in reality or meet someone through friends and we do have great chemistry and a lot of flirtation, then we do go on a date, they end up being the

> *kind of guys who just want sex, are not great listeners, and don't*
> *really want to actually have anything real. Why am I so much*
> *more attracted to people who seem to not want commitment*
> *than the people who actually have their values aligned with mine*
> *and want to have the same things as me?*

The answer to this question is so much simpler than it seems. This person is responding to a familiar feeling of attraction but yearning for a different result. The chemistry you are drawn to is actually your body's way of telling you that it recognizes a similarity in this person. It's not even necessarily attraction, it's familiarity. For this letter writer, the way these guys flirt, the way they give her the eye from across the room, all of it is signaling a similar adrenaline boost that she's gotten from flirting with similar men. But then she gets a similar response: they flirt with her, take her out, then ask if she's DTF (which means "down to F").

From my vantage point, I can see an invisible line that this person is drawing between those she meets online and those she meets through friends. If you're similar to this letter writer, dating apps are the place you try to date with intention, but when you date IRL (in real life), you toss away all of the dating preparation that you've done. This person is able to resist the f*ckboys online because she's in an intentional mindset there, but she's not evaluating the men she meets casually by the same standards. Second, it sounds like this person is going on dates with people who share her goals and values, but she's tossing them out as viable options when the sparks don't develop right away.

Does this happen in your dating life, too? What would happen if you traded chemistry for curiosity? What would happen if you followed the Three Date Rule and gave the connection time to unfold?

THE THREE DATE RULE

One way of taking your time and practicing slow love is by abiding by the Three Date Rule. Even though each relationship develops on its own timeline, my clients insist on a few guidelines on timing, so here goes. My Three Date Rule states that you give any person three dates as long as you are still curious about them. If no sexual chemistry develops by the third date, then you can let it go, knowing you gave true romance its best shot. Now for the inevitable follow-up FAQs:

But, Damona, what if they are rude or offensive?

Of course you shouldn't go out with them again. If they behave inappropriately or make you feel embarrassed or uncomfortable, that's not how you should feel in a relationship.

But, Damona, what if they are really unattractive?

As in, there is nothing about them that is at all attractive internally or externally? I've seen clients who didn't initially feel a physical attraction develop it by the third date, but you have to give in to your curiosity to get there. If you don't have that, you have nothing.

But, Damona, what if they have one of my deal breakers?

Remember that goals and values are the biggest predictors of long-term compatibility, so if you're not aligned there, even if you have butterflies, even if you have the best conversation you've ever had on a date, you're probably fooling yourself. Whether you're telling yourself you need to give them the benefit of the doubt or you just like a challenge, you know how this story is going to end.

But, Damona, what if I liked them, but their shoes were a total turnoff?

C'mon.

CHEMISTRY CASE STUDY: JOGGERS GUY

My friend Devyn Simone, a fantastic matchmaker, dating coach, and TV personality, shared the story on *Dates & Mates* of meeting her man for the first time. They had a great time, but she couldn't get over the fact that he wore joggers on a first date. To her, it indicated a lack of care or legitimate interest in the date. She went so far as to joke in a post-date message: "It was nice meeting you . . . and your pants," punctuating the sting with the pants emoji 👖.

They went their separate ways until years later when they reconnected on Clubhouse, the audio-driven social media app. They made a connection and took the conversation off the app. Exchanging phone numbers unearthed their previous texts. This was "joggers guy." Intrigued by their Clubhouse conversations, she went out with him anyway and discovered that everything she believed about the joggers was false. The real story was that he'd spilled coffee on the pants he was going to wear on the date and had to make a choice to cancel or wear the joggers from his gym bag. He figured it was better to show up in joggers than not at all. He wore better pants when they met up the next time, and within a few weeks, they were both off the dating market.

> *Dear Damona,*
> *I went out with a gorgeous woman yesterday and I really want to see her again, but I don't want to seem overeager. What's the best way to let her know that I'm interested and I'm serious?*

Many dating coaches will tell you to play it cool and not tip your hand, but I think dating is far too competitive today to keep it casual if you meet someone who piques your interest. The old rule was to wait three days to call. In three days, she could have seventy-five matches and forty-two messages from other people who aren't afraid to share their feelings or be assertive. You lose nothing by telling someone how you feel. Just remember, you have limited information after one date, so you don't know the future. One date can't tell you whether they are perfect for you or whether you're destined to be together, but it can tell you that you want to see them again. So, say just that: "I had a really great time with you and I'd love to see you again." We are viewed as overeager only if the feeling isn't mutual. And the only way you can figure that out is by bravely communicating what you're feeling.

CHEMISTRY CASE STUDY: THE THIRD DATE THAT ALMOST WASN'T

A coaching client of mine, Danielle, had gone through my program focused on dating with intention and committed to dating differently. She matched with a guy on an app who wasn't her usual type. They had a great first date full of curiosity and connection.

He was going to be in her neighborhood for work, so they made a plan to meet for a drink in the early evening for a second date. The bar they picked was bustling with the happy hour crowd. She pushed through the half-wasted worker bees blowing off steam and snagged them the most secluded table she could find. She waited. And waited.

Finally, he burst through the door, still in his suit from work, a little frazzled that he was late. He seemed stiff, distracted, and aloof. That magical chemistry she'd felt on the first date had vanished.

Our next session, she questioned whether she should take him up on that third date. After such an awkward second date, she began to wonder whether what she felt the first time was real and she almost pulled the plug. I reminded her about the Three Date Rule.

I asked her, "Are you still curious about him?" She immediately answered yes. All of this turmoil was driven by insecurity that he might have lost interest in her, he might not be committed enough, he might just not be The One. That's making the second date do far too much work. She didn't need to know the answer to the big question at that point. She just needed to determine whether she was willing to spend another hour or two with him.

Danielle reported that the sparks were back on the third date and by the time she finished my three-month program, they'd made it official. It turns out he'd had a bad day at work and felt horrible about being late to their second date. All the time she was worrying that he wasn't interested in her, he was wondering the same thing and assuming he'd blown it.

So many arbitrary elements can factor into chemistry. It could be joggers, it could be the lighting, it could be someone's tone of voice, it could be the way they walk or their smile. The difference between chemistry and connection is that chemistry is a chemical reaction and, therefore, it fades over time. Connection *deepens* the longer you know someone.

THE COMMUNICATION CRISIS

Let's not get ahead of ourselves, though. I would love to counsel more people on second and third dates, but the reality is that most people who write into *Dates & Mates* are hitting a dating wall well before that point. Either they never make it past the first date or they can't even seem to make it to the point of meeting up with anyone offline at all. You might think that the overwhelming number of match possibilities at daters' literal fingertips is leaving people indecisive. That's part of it, but there is something much bigger going on right now: the communication crisis.

We have constant chatter happening in our lives as a result of the expansion of our social circle online and the number of people whose updates are populating our feed. We have Slack notifications, overflowing inboxes, a never-ending stream of text messages, and Zoom meeting after in-person meeting after Skype. With so much conversation, you might think we are more connected than ever, but the absolute opposite is true. Our constant connectedness is creating a communication crisis where we have so much information coming in that we are losing the meaning of each individual message.

This is why so many people are experiencing dating burnout. We are constantly talking, but no one is saying anything. If you're feeling this, it's vitally important that you create some structure around your dating life. With the speed and volume of messaging increasing, if you don't have a process to manage your notifications, your communication, and your dates, you can easily get sucked into the dating void.

Don't be afraid to take dating breaks when you need them. However, I recommend that you set a time to reenter the dating scene with intention. Otherwise, you might end up ignoring dating entirely only to sloppily throw together a profile in a wine-fueled moment of weakness a few months from now.

If you're mindfully dating, choose whom you wish to communicate with and give them your proper attention. Don't feel obligated to chat with everyone who messages you because that will deplete your energy for the connections you actually want to foster. But remember to show compassion toward those who are not a match. Closing the loop with them conserves your energy and allows them the mental freedom to pursue someone else as well.

It's also worth noting that the apps can monitor who is writing back, how long conversations last on the app, and who is swiping right on everyone but ignoring messages once they come in. Apps of all kinds want active users, and dating apps operate the same way. Those who are responsive are rewarded algorithmically.

> *Dear Damona,*
> *I heard you say on the podcast that women should send messages, but doesn't that make men lazy? I work so hard at the office, I don't want to come home and do more work in dating.*

Because we already put The Rules to bed, we won't spend too much time reviewing the idea that there are no gender rules for who messages first online, but just in case you are still questioning it, I'll offer you a little data. OkCupid reports that conversations among heterosexual daters last twice as long when women initiate than when men do. Still, many daters are applying 1950s gender roles to modern dating app messaging. The data show that it doesn't really matter who messages or matches first. If you're interested, just go for it!

Dating with intention shouldn't feel like work—at least not like the same kind of work you do at the office. See the opportunity in it to get more of what you want by doing the choosing instead of waiting around to "get chosen."

I will never subscribe to the trending belief that dating apps make men (or daters of any gender, for that matter) lazy. However, I do think that dating apps can make people exhausted if we're fielding messages from too many people, chatting on them for entertainment without intention behind it, and just sitting around waiting for chemistry to strike and the perfect match to land in our inbox. Remember that the dating app is just a piece of technology designed to create introductions. It does not have feelings, it does not have opinions, and, most of all, it does not have a gender.

CONFLICT RESOLUTION

Let's say you've gone through the three dates and want to keep going. The next step after curiosity and communication is conflict resolution. It's what the first-date banter will eventually evolve into, because not one relationship has avoided all speed bumps on the way to long-term happiness. You're going to encounter friction at some point in the relationship (and not only of the sexy variety). Conflict resolution style can be the greatest indicator of how compatible two people will be in the long run. Real conflict cannot be tackled over text; we have to endure those uncomfortable face-to-face conversations.

When there is a breakdown in communication, trust, or understanding, psychologists call this a rupture. We tend to fixate on the rupture. We tell our friends about it and we post it on social media, yet we fear going in to try to fix it because that presents the potential for more pain. For growth and healing, after each rupture, you need to also experience the repair. A repair is when you learn how your words or actions impact someone else and you uplevel yourself and your communication skills by fixing the damage the rupture caused.

You can't avoid conflict altogether. Trying to do so only keeps you walking on eggshells or stuffing your feelings away. On the other side of the coin, you need to pick your battles. If everything is a conflict, you both will be frustrated and exhausted. Yet finding your voice in your relationship and learning how to communicate your needs is more fulfilling than any screaming match you could ever have. Understanding how your partner communicates and resolves conflict is the key to unlocking the next level in your relationship.

Coming from a Black, Jewish household, I learned to solve my problems loudly. Actually, my family does everything at full volume. My husband has a much quieter nature and a mother who was a social worker and who founded a shelter for victims of domestic violence when he was an infant. All this to say, he was used to talking things out quietly and calmly. It took months for me to realize that, although I felt better shouting and getting all my emotions out, it was unsettling to him and made him retreat from the conversation. I had to learn to listen more and bring down my voice a few decibels. He had to learn to speak up and tell me when my tone was pushing us further from a resolution. What makes this work is a shared desire to grow into a healthy conflict resolution style with one another.

The Gottman Institute has identified five kinds of conflict styles in couples:

1. Conflict avoiders: Rather than trying to persuade the other of their point of view, these couples seek common ground in a conflict. This type of couple has a healthy balance of being independent and interdependent, supported by their ability to keep clear boundaries.
2. Volatile: Couples with this style love to debate but seem to approach it as all in good fun. They do not insult one another and they emphasize connection and honesty in their conflicts.
3. Validating: In this style, couples seek commonality. They are empathetic toward their partner and strive to understand their partner's point of view in a conflict.

This couple tends to stay calm in their conflicts and avoid confronting their differences.

4. Hostile: This style is marked by a lot of criticism in conflict and difficulty seeing their partner's point of view. During conflicts, couples with this style tend to reiterate their point of view without making an effort to offer support or understand their partner's perspective.

5. Hostile-detached: In this style, the couple stays emotionally detached from one another. In their conflicts, all of what Dr. Gottman calls the Four Horsemen are present: criticism, contempt, defensiveness, and stonewalling. These four qualities are bad omens of relationship instability and can push partners away.

Though they look vastly different, what the first three conflict styles share is a "magic ratio" of positive interactions to negative ones of five to one. This means that for every negative interaction, there are five or more positive interactions. By examining conflict resolution styles, Dr. John Gottman could predict the likelihood of divorce in the couples he studied with 90 percent accuracy.

If you are finding the number of conflicts you and your partner have differs greatly from the "magic ratio," especially early on, run! Or employ more empathy. Making sure your partner feels heard and understood is the first step in learning to resolve conflict.

Second, find opportunities for agreement. You might not be able to be on the same page about everything, but if you look for the common ground, you can build from there.

Finally, be affectionate. No, I'm not talking about makeup sex. You can express physical affection for your partner, such as by touching their hand or offering a hug, when you're discussing something difficult or as part of the repair process after a rupture. Physical affection helps you rebuild connection without having to find the perfect words to say.

The problem with looking for the perfect words to say is that there are no perfect words. Clear communication requires you to have clarity on what you're trying to express first but also you have to have compassion for your partner as you listen to their point of view. I love the question "Do you want to be right or do you want to be happy?" Of course I want to be both and I assume you do, too, but as you're looking for that balance, the best thing you can be is honest.

chapter 10

F chemistry, fix your dates

BEFORE WE CAN GET INTO TIPS FOR THE ACTUAL DATE, WE have to talk about what you're doing before you get to the date. If you aren't prepared, and if you're not in the right mental space before you get to the date, you're not setting yourself up for success. Instead of thinking of it as one more thing to do, think of preparation as a step that will actually save you time and energy because you will be able to relax and be your most authentic self.

PRE-DATE RITUAL

You need a pre-date ritual to get excited, focused, and in the right headspace to do your best on that date. What makes you feel at ease? For me, it was always (and still is) exercise. Prior to a date,

I would usually try to work in a few minutes at the gym. I would rather show up a little dewy than nervous and anxious. If you sweat heavily, this might not be the play for you, or you might want to build in time for a shower or a quick trip home.

Another great pre-date ritual is listening to music. I encourage all my clients to create pre-date playlists with different vibes depending on the energy they want to cultivate.

Other clients have found solace in phoning a friend before the date—just make sure it's your hype man and not your negative Nancy. Sorry, Nancy, nothing personal.

You can take a walk around the block, practice yoga, do a crossword puzzle, pet your cat, listen to your favorite podcast, dance around the room, or read a book. Choose your own pre-date ritual adventure. As long as it shifts your energy and brings you into the mental and emotional state you'd like to take with you into the date, it works.

Consider a clothing change if you're meeting up after work. Even if it's just adding earrings or slipping on a different pair of shoes, that can make a big difference in shifting your energy from work mode to date mode. It's not about getting into your "feminine or masculine energy," as some dating experts will tell you. It's about leaving the details and emotions that don't belong on the date at home and starting the date on a level, energetic playing field.

PRE-DATE SCREENING

How much research is too much? If there's something you're dying to discuss with your date but you can't because you found it out in a secret Instagram rabbit hole, you've gone too far. If you're bursting at the seams, worried you're going to slip up and reveal the secret information you've gathered on them, you've painted yourself into a corner.

A basic Google search, however, is appropriate for safety in today's climate. Some apps have even incorporated background checks to give you peace of mind. Security is important, but overresearching robs you of the opportunity to discover the person in real time.

My favorite pre-date screening activity has always been a phone call. Don't give out your real phone number, though; get a dating burner phone. Then you can feel like a sexy spy and have a secondary phone number that can't be tracked back to your address or personal information and that you can cancel if you have a date that's a little too communicative.

I prefer a phone call over a video chat because it's less intimate and preserves some of the anticipation for the date. Yet a phone call can still show you what your date's energy is like and how good your banter will be in person. Postpandemic, we became so comfortable with video conferences that many people are trading a phone call for a video call. I will reluctantly agree to get on board with this trend as long as you follow a few ground rules.

THE ART OF THE VIRTUAL DATE

Just as texting has changed the way we communicate prior to the date, the accessibility and quality of video chat software has also made a meaningful impact on the dating process. When I started my podcast eleven years ago, I became a regular Skype user. It had come a long way from its launch in 2003, when I watched glitchy video interviews on *The Oprah Winfrey Show* being celebrated for being delivered by a Skype connection. It was cutting-edge at the time.

Over the years, the technology improved, and through video chat, I was able to interview people who otherwise couldn't make it into my studio in Los Angeles. It always felt like we had a real connection because I could take in the entire context of what they were saying through body language, facial expressions, and even the room they were broadcasting from. I even began my role on *The Drew Barrymore Show* from my home studio in the middle of the pandemic. Without video chat, our show would never have been able to go on.

So, when my client Tess called to say she'd met someone who lived on the other side of the country, I was ready with my long-distance dating strategy. It worked and she ended up moving, getting engaged, and building a new life in his city.

In 2020, when in-person conversation was eliminated, everyone turned to Zoom and other video-conferencing tools to stay connected, ones I had already been using for over a decade. Dating apps raced to add video chat features, and dating quickly became 100 percent virtual. Many people rushed into online situationships. Scores of them broke up months later and I wished I could have reached them with my long-distance dating strategy before it was too late.

The setup of a virtual date varies based on the purpose. If you are using it as a screening step to determine whether or not you want to move offline with someone, here are a few helpful guidelines that have led my clients to success:

Lighting is your friend. Having the right lighting can be the difference between looking like a movie star and looking like a serial killer. Try to have natural light on your face. If that's not possible, pick up a ring light or find a place where you have flattering lighting already. Not sure if it's flattering? Take a screenshot and send it to your most honest friend. Or to my daughter. She tells it like it is (whether you want to hear it or not).

What's that lurking behind you? A virtual background can be seen as creepy since people might think you're trying to hide something, but you don't want to air all of your dirty laundry (literally) for your date. Everything in the frame is part of how they will perceive you, so pay attention to where you sit and what's in the background. Ideally, you want to find a comfortable place in your home where you won't have to put up a folding screen, which is even more creepy than a virtual one. And perhaps you leave a little mystery and make them work up to the bed.

Go handsfree. If you're using a phone or tablet, get a stand or tripod so you can relax and not have to hold your device for the entire conversation.

Keep it short and sweet. If this is not a replacement for an actual date but rather a screening step to decide whether you want to meet them or not, aim for thirty minutes or less. It will not feel abrupt to cut it off if you are telling them you want to meet in person. Yet if you know from the video conversation that you don't want to meet up, most people appreciate a clear no and will value earning their time back rather than trying to convince you to change your mind.

If you're meeting someone long distance, however, different rules apply beyond the first meetup. I've seen a major uptick in long-distance relationships (LDRs). As outlined in the Introduction, thanks to travel and technology, new relationships are able to thrive across the miles.

My client Christina admitted that being a long distance away from her fiancé is probably what enabled their relationship to thrive. She came to me with the assumption that she didn't really intend to ever get married but with a goal of finding companionship. After months of having fun with my techniques and going on countless first and second dates, she met someone while she was on vacation. He was in town only for a short while as well and he lived in another country—not exactly the building blocks of a long-term relationship. Christina didn't intend to fall in love, but they stayed in touch across the miles and over time their bond deepened. She also credits the distance with imposing slow love and setting the sexual exploration of their relationship on simmer while the emotional exploration sizzled. Flipping the ratio of those interactions helped them develop a deep bond and even changed her outlook on marriage.

Here are some guidelines for keeping connection in an LDR:

Plan actual dates. Many long-distance daters fall into a casual connection very quickly. Nightly check-ins can make you feel comfortable and connected but can extinguish the spark within a few weeks. Put virtual dates on the calendar so that you can look forward to them. Plan a virtual dinner where you both pick up the same food and eat together as if you're in a restaurant. Take your partner on a virtual tour of your neighborhood. Play an online game together. These kinds of activities require more planning but keep the spark alive the same way they would if you were spacing out your in-person dates.

Tell, don't show. Keeping up regular communication with a long-distance partner is important. With social media giving an intimate window into our daily lives, you never want your partner to feel like a spectator standing on the sidelines of your life. Loop them in about your plans so they're not blindsided by a 2:00 a.m. Instagram story that shows you having the time of your life without them.

Put it on the calendar. Even if you stay up all night talking or video chatting and you feel like they know everything about your life, it's still not real until you meet in person. My client Daisy fell in love with someone overseas. Everyone in her life thought she was crazy when she announced that she'd be taking a fourteen-hour journey to spend a week with her online love just six weeks after meeting. I did not. I told her she had to go and she had to see whether this connection was real before she invested more time and emotional energy. She took the trip and eight months later he moved to the States and they were married. Maybe the stakes aren't as extreme for you, but even if you're a short flight or drive away, you need to make the effort to be together in person regularly to see whether the magic remains when you're dealing with the mundane details of daily life.

THE DATE TRACKER

I'll admit, I'm not an organized person, but I find that organization really serves my clients in dating because we can track what is working, record thoughts and feelings along the way, and fine-tune the experience to get to our ultimate goal. I laughed out loud when a woman went viral on TikTok for keeping an Excel spreadsheet of her dates. Apparently, TikTok was not aware of Amy Webb, the author of *Data, a Love Story*, who explained how she used her background as a data-driven futurist to compute her online dating success on spreadsheets over a decade ago. If TikTok didn't know that then, it definitely didn't know that I had been encouraging my clients to track their online dating experiences since I began coaching. I have a full workbook in my Dating Accelerator Program, but if you're not enrolled in that yet, a simple dating journal is a good starting point.

Start with tracking which pre-date rituals work for you. Then, take note of the following things after your date:

- How you felt emotionally going into the date
- What your energy level was during the date
- How much focus you had throughout the date

Every time I wrote a Date Lab article for the *Washington Post*, I'd tell the participants prior to the date to make notes about their date as soon as they got home so the details would be clear when we did the interview later. About half of the folks I interviewed did this and half of them either forgot or told themselves that they'd still remember the details a day or two later. It's amazing how our memories work, especially if we've been drinking. When the interviewees had not written notes, they often didn't recall the topics of conversation until I prompted them with the common date subjects or details that the other participant had shared in their interview. Simply the act of writing something down can help you commit the details to memory, even if you never refer back to your dating journal. This process is helpful when you're on the fence about going out again or when you're juggling multiple dating options (which hopefully will be the case after you finish this book).

Here are some questions to answer in your dating journal that will give you a better understanding of what really happened and what's next:

1. **Are you curious?** Is there more that you'd like to know about who they are, how they were raised, or what they want in life?
2. **Are you aligned in values?** You don't necessarily need to have the same exact beliefs, but are your core values at least compatible?
3. **Do you share the same goals?** Do you both want something serious or something casual? What is your relationship timeline? Are your lives generally headed in the same direction?
4. **Does your gut say yes?** We have thousands of nerve endings in our stomach. We need to start to honor the validity of going with your gut feeling.

If your answer to three out of four of the questions above is yes, you owe them and yourself another date. It's amazing what we can talk ourselves into and out of, but when you see the facts on the paper in front of you, and you've done the foundational work to get clarity on what your relationship needs truly are, you can relax into your choice and remain in the moment with the person before you.

HOW LONG SHOULD A FIRST DATE BE?

The first date should be only about sixty minutes (ninety minutes *tops*). A longer date usually ends with you revealing things about yourself that are too intimate, finding out more about your date than you needed to know, or having three too many mojitos (or so I've heard).

Keep that initial interaction short and sweet, and prepare yourself for an exit and an entrance. I mean quite literally you should be coming from somewhere (so you have something to talk about upon arrival) and going to somewhere (even if it's home to feed your fish), giving you an exit strategy before you even begin the date. It's important that you give the date a set end time and communicate it beforehand. This way, it doesn't feel abrupt or rude when you end the date at sixty minutes either because you're not having a great time or because you want to leave something more to be revealed.

The energy of a first date is like a wave. We always start high because we are excited to meet someone new and nervous about getting on their wavelength. Then we go through a few peaks and valleys as we cycle through different topics of conversation. Eventually, if you let the date go long enough, you will get tired and run out of things to say and the energy will start to fall.

That's when the date flatlines. Instead, end the date feeling like you've paused in the middle, leaving more to be discovered.

What we remember most about dates are the beginning and the ending. I couldn't tell you one topic that my husband and I discussed on our first date, but I remember the moment I first saw him and I remember him walking me to my car at the end of the night. I'll tell you why I remembered that later. . . .

End the date when you're still on a high note. That kind of energy is the stuff second dates are made of. Leave them wanting more (and leave yourself with curiosity as the person before you opens up and reveals themself to you).

WHERE TO GO AND WHAT TO DO

There is no perfect date location, but I do recommend developing a regular rotation of date venues where you feel safe and comfortable and that are close to home.

You certainly will have to meet dates halfway or go to them every now and then, but you should always have an answer at the ready when your date asks you where you like to go.

DAMONA'S BEST DATE SPOTS

1. Bars

Hands down, bars are built for dating. The lighting is soft enough to blur the rough edges of an awkward meetup. A drink or two is often settling for the nerves and the seating is ideal. Catty-corner positioning is close enough to feel intimate or even touch one another if it comes to that. You also can have an eye outward to take in other stimuli that can add to the conversation, and it won't feel like a job interview, with intense eye contact sitting across the table face-to-face.

I know some of you are thinking, *But, Damona, what if I don't drink?* If you're comfortable with being in a bar and having a nonalcoholic drink, you don't have to make a scene. If a bar is not your venue, that's fine. Teetotalers actually make up a larger part of the population than most people think and a growing number of OkCupid users are indulging in the dry dating trend. In 2022, there was a 14 percent increase in people adding the word *sober* to their profiles. Even some people who drink are choosing to stay sober for first dates, so you can just tell your date you don't drink or just order a Sprite and it doesn't have to be an issue if you don't make it one.

2. Activity Places

This is a huge category of date spots that encompasses everything from hiking to museums to arcades or golf (mini or otherwise). An activity date gives you a shared experience and helps you form a memory together while also keeping you from stressing out about date conversation topics. An added benefit, if you do something that boosts your endorphins, you actually will bring a higher energy to the date and trigger the same hormones that are released when you fall in love. Voila—relationship shortcut.

3. Coffee Shops, Ice Cream Shops, Cutesy Eateries

Coffee shops aren't just for day dates any more. Although day dates are deeply underrated, they actually are gaining momentum. The benefit of a day date is you can bring a fresh energy to the table and you have less work, family, pet, life stress to carry with you. Don't just pick any old coffee shop or ice cream parlor, though. Having side-hustled through college as a Starbucks barista, I know that each location has a different vibe, so you have to find the spots with the best atmosphere for a date. Look for places with comfortable seating, where you can re-create the bar's catty-corner positioning. Also pay attention to the noise level at the time you'll be there and make sure you can hear one another.

LOCATION, LOCATION, LOCATIONS?

I know people love to keep the energy of a date going. They think that if the connection is good, they should stay on the date for as long as possible. Not only does this have notes of desperation and fear—that if you let them go, they'll never come back—it also doesn't achieve the goal of ending on a high note. Most importantly, a second location often ends up with more drinking, fuzzier decision-making, and too much personal sharing. Get out when the getting is good.

WHO ARE YOU WEARING?

In our post-date interviews nearly all of the people I interviewed and wrote about in the *Washington Post* Date Lab columns included a mention of selecting their clothing or noticing what their date is wearing. The level of stress that people put themselves through over choosing the right shade of denim is not only unnecessary but also takes their eye off the ball. When that energy should be directed toward your pre-date ritual, you are running around like a maniac asking your roommate if you should go with prints or solids.

Prepare yourself before the date by trying on a number of potential date outfits and setting aside two to three looks for various types of dates. In my early dating workshops with Match .com, my stylist Lori Ann Robinson and I coined the term "dating capsule wardrobe" for the set of date looks that you could reliably turn to.

Look 1—Fancy: Dinner, cocktails, or an activity that's a little bit elevated, a fancy look helps set the scene for the date you imagine.

Look 2—Casual: Grabbing beers, meeting for ice cream or pub trivia. This is the best comfortable, casual version of yourself.

Look 3—Athletic: If you're going hiking or rock climbing or doing something outdoorsy with your date, you need an outfit that you can move in and of course appropriate footwear.

That's it! You really only need three basic looks for dating. I know someone who decided to approach dating as an experiment. She planned to do a hundred dates at the same location wearing the same outfit so the only factor that was changing was the guy. One of my clients was date number 97. She called the experiment off and now they are married with three children.

Once you have your core dating capsule wardrobe, you can think about preparing for the specific date at hand.

a. Consider the weather and have contingency outfits planned depending on the forecast.

b. Imagine or inquire about which activities you might do on the date. If there's a chance that you could be walking a long distance, make sure you have your walking shoes. I keep a pair of flip-flops or flats in my bag so I can burst into a sprint at any moment. Okay, I'm exaggerating about the sprint, but I did have a Date Lab participant who failed to account for game-day parking and ended up circling to find a lot and huffing it in heels several blocks to make it to her date location. If you fail to prepare you prepare to fail, or at least to be sweaty and inconvenienced with blistered feet. Not a sexy way to start your date.

c. Do the sit test. We tend to only look at what we are wearing while standing up in the mirror, which is cute if you're going to be on your feet the entire date, but if you plan on sitting down, you'd better test it out. Can you breathe? Can you eat? Can you sit there and look nice without constantly tugging on buttons and belts? Comfort is key.

CONVERSATION PIECE CLOTHING

It's so hard to start a conversation with a stranger. One simple thing that can ease you into a connection is wearing "conversation piece clothing." This is an item of clothing or an accessory that has a story attached to it or one that simply stands out. Anything can be a conversation piece of clothing if it creates conversation around it.

One of the Date Lab participants that we matched in the column said he always wore a Hawaiian-style shirt with bananas on it to his dates. We have the photographic proof that his Date Lab night was no exception. He told me in our interview that he wore it because it was his most disarming shirt. His date said with approval, "He looked like someone who didn't take himself too seriously." Ultimately, they had a ton in common (I mean, they did have a great matchmaker), but the conversation piece shirt got the ball rolling.

FLIRT SCHOOL

Flirty is probably the last adjective you ever would have used to describe me before 1998. I was not one of the girls in high school who guys would flirt with or ask on dates. In fact, I asked both my junior and senior prom dates to attend with me (including the first junior prom date, who canceled three days before, and the second junior prom date, who told me within the first five minutes that he knew I really wanted to be there with the other guy). Whatever "it" was, I didn't have it.

Many years later, I had a crush on a guy that I worked with and I really wanted him to notice me. Because we worked together, even though there was no formal policy against dating at the company, I didn't want to be too obvious about my interest. Subtly, I'd try to flirt through facial expressions, my tone of voice, playful topics of conversation, and what I wore. I finally caught his eye long enough to learn that he had a girlfriend and we would have to stop flirting with each other, but at that point a lightbulb went off for me. Though I was unsuccessful at landing a date in this situation, I was successful in conveying my interest in someone.

I concluded that flirts are not born, they're made. We figure out how to flirt by testing out various actions and then noticing the reaction we receive. I can't teach a one-size-fits-all approach to flirting, but I can give you techniques and tools that I now use with clients to help them find a flirtatious approach that is comfortable for them.

Ultimately, flirting is about confidence. You must have the confidence to express what you want and the courage to know that you can still stand in your personal power even though it might not land the way you intend (or you might find out they have a girlfriend).

IMPROVE WITH IMPROV

If you've ever been to an improv show, you know that no one is more confident and expressive than an improv performer. That is why I use the foundations of improv to teach my clients how to be more confident on dates and flirt like the pros.

There are three main elements of improv that are foundational in flirting coaching:

1. Listening
2. Storytelling
3. Body language

LISTENING

Daters come to me with so much fear about what to say on dates to make them seem charming and funny. But dating is not a stand-up comedy set, where the performer talks *at* you. It's more like improv in that the performers are interacting with one another to create a totally unique and often amusing shared experience.

Most people think they are good listeners, but both dating and improv share a different kind of listening. Rather than just listening for content—meaning the specifics of what someone says—daters should be listening for engagement.

When you're watching an improv show, the performers aren't only tracking the details of the story that is unfolding but also listening, knowing that they are going to have to interact with the information that is being shared. They will build on what came first as the show goes on and they are working as a team with their fellow players.

When you are listening with intent, your mind is in the moment. If you project into the future or ruminate on the past, you will miss what's happening in the now. A core improv exercise that can help you achieve that is "Yes, And."

"Yes, And" is often one of the first exercises improvisers learn because it helps them generate a connection with their partner. The exercise has the same effect in dating. Let's consider the *yes* first. Because you are creating a completely new imaginative scenario each time, in improv, everything you say is correct. If you negate what your partner says, you are preventing the story from unfolding and pitting yourself against your partner rather than bringing them into the conversation with you. Therefore, in the

"Yes, And" exercise, you listen to what your partner says and reply *yes* to the statement that they just made, then you say *and* and add on to the story.

I start my clients with "Yes, And" in the same way. They sit across from my flirting coach, who begins the exercise by making a statement, and no matter how off the wall it might be, the client says *yes* to it, thereby affirming their partner's choice and helping build confidence in the connection. Next, they say *and*, then add additional information to the story. They volley back and forth like this until they have a sense that they are cocreating an experience with my flirting coach.

Once my client has mastered that skill, we move on to making it real in a "Trading Personal Stories" exercise. In a similar fashion, my flirting coach starts with a personal story and the client must say *yes* to it *and* add on a personal story from their own life. This gets my client used to listening with intent and looking for ways to reveal details about themselves.

The personal story you share can be anything that is inspired by what the other person has said. While the flirting coach might be telling a story about riding the Ferris wheel at a carnival, the client might not have a relevant story to share about rides. So, instead, they might say, "Yes, and carnivals always remind me of summer. We would spend our summers on road trips with our parents." Once they are more comfortable with making the connections and sharing their stories, we take out the "Yes, And," and it begins to feel more like an actual date, with easy banter flowing back and forth.

Now the number one question I get about this exercise is, "When I say 'Yes, And,' does that mean I have to agree with what my date says all the time?" Of course not! The *yes* in a date scenario is, first of all, unspoken and, second of all, simply an acknowledgment that you hear the other person; it makes them feel safe sharing their stories.

STORYTELLING

The other purpose of teaching my clients improv is to get them more comfortable with storytelling. Again, this is a skill that some people are naturally gifted at, but most people can learn to improve.

The best way to get better at telling stories is to tell more stories. An improv exercise that I use for this is called "Press Conference." My client is told they're an expert in a topic and they will be giving a press conference. They need to speak confidently about this topic for two minutes and then answer questions from the audience, which is usually other students or my flirting coach. The more absurd the topic, the better, because my client has to be able to speak with confidence and answer questions with authority. When we start in a ridiculous scenario where they can just play and have fun with the topic, it's easier for them to play expert. Often, we become nervous about sharing our own stories, but making up stories and answers is easier in a made-up scenario. In time, that confidence can transfer to telling your own stories and sharing your personal details without fear of judgment.

From there, we move on to "Personal Story off of a Suggestion." We give the client a random topic and they must confidently tell a story from their own lives that involves it. This mimics the exact scenario they will encounter on a date. You can do this preparation and improve your improv and flirting skills, but you have no idea what the date will bring to the table. If you can build your confidence and ability to connect different stories from your life to a topic, you can handle pretty much any question or conversation thread that comes your way on a date.

As you graduate to actual date conversation techniques, try to ask questions that get your date to tell a story rather than give simple one-word responses. Also, tapping into any nostalgic stories or stories of similar experiences can help you feel more aligned.

An example: Rather than asking what kind of music they are into (a remarkably common question on a date), ask about the first concert they attended or the most recent concert they saw. That can tell you about the style of music they like, how their interests have evolved, who they spend time with, and more. Plus, music makes us nostalgic in itself. People with memory loss can often remember the lyrics to songs that were popular in their youth despite being unable to remember anything else about their current lives.

Although you weren't at the same concert, you might know that album and remember a time when you listened to it or what a particular song meant to you. Now, instead of going into a robotic trade of information, you are actually layering stories and connections with one another.

Tapping into nostalgia can immediately bond you and a stranger as you trigger a memory that feels familiar to them. If you talk to someone about going to a particular movie or what lunchtime was like at your school, they'll automatically think of going to the movies in their hometown or lunchtime at their school as their mind tries to picture the event you're describing. Even though you may have grown up in totally different places, there is a feeling of sameness that emerges from recalling parallel experiences.

BODY LANGUAGE

Another parallel experience you can share is physical: a mirroring exercise. Next time you're out with good friends, take notice of your movements and vocal cues. You'll likely see that you are mirroring one another without even realizing it. When you are connecting with someone, you automatically begin to mirror them. This might mean subconsciously mimicking verbal cues: tone of voice, pace of speaking, or choice of vocabulary. You might also subtly mirror their body language without even realizing it: talking with your hands, leaning in, sitting closer, crossing your legs or arms, or tapping your fingers. I want to spare my clients the embarrassment of trying to do a mime routine with a stranger, but mirroring, when done correctly, is an excellent technique to build rapport on a date.

Here's where it gets weird. If you mirror your date's cues to signify interest, they can sometimes feel a connection, even if they can't explain why. Social psychologists refer to this unconscious mirroring effect as the Gauchais reaction and they believe it is hard-wired in us from birth when babies first learn to read and match the facial and body language cues of their caretakers. Limbic synchrony, as it is also called, can happen naturally, but it can be done with intent and generate the same outcome. Most of us already employ limbic synchrony in business situations or when dealing with challenging people with whom we need to build rapport or disarm from a defensive position. What's more challenging than a first date? This technique is not a magic trick and won't make someone fall for you. That's a fairy-tale myth and I told you to dump those chapters ago. However, if someone is on the fence or if they find you attractive but aren't feeling that special something, mirroring can turn a maybe into a yes.

One of my biggest goals when I'm running flirting trainings is to get daters out of their heads and into their bodies. If you are too practiced or too strategic in your conversation technique, it will feel forced for both of you and prevent you from being able to connect with your date. Ninety percent of communication is nonverbal, so the most important thing you can do on a date is to show up comfortable in your body and able to express yourself both verbally and physically.

SET IT UP

The simplest flirting technique that I teach daters is to SET It Up.

Smile: Not only does smiling change your neurochemistry, but also smiling can actually ward off depression and induce feelings of joy. Plus, it is comforting and disarming to a date. It gives them the impression that you enjoy their company, which will put them at ease.

Eye contact: You don't want to stare down your date's soul, but at the same time you want to give them the impression that you are interested in what they have to say, and the simplest way to signify this is by looking at them more than you look away, more than you check out the person at the next table, and definitely more than you check your phone.

Touch: Touch is a powerful escalator on dates. Even a simple graze of the hand or touch on the shoulder can take you from zero to sixty, so use touch sparingly and with consent. Asking someone if you can hold their hand or kiss them before you reach out to do it is way sexier than pouncing on an unwilling participant. If you have any concerns about asking for consent or think that it ruins the mood, then you probably haven't actually tried it in a while. Next time, please do. Notice I said *please*. See how pleasant manners and consent can be?

BUT IS THE FLAG ACTUALLY RED OR GREEN?

Over the last year, the most common topic I've been asked to discuss on TV is dating red flags. Everyone is looking for a universal sign to tell whether they're talking to a deadbeat or whether the date they have on Friday is going to ghost them. Although I have given out a few tips on red flags around dating safety, catfish profiles, and horrible first date traits, I've come to the conclusion that we should really be talking about dating green flags. We can always find a reason to eliminate someone, but if we focus our attention on reasons to say yes, we can usually move the date from being transactional to being more meaningful.

What's that? You get my point about the green flags but you still want to hear the red flags? The heart wants what the heart wants, so here we go.

RED FLAGS OF DATING SAFETY

The Tinder Swindler burst on the scene and online daters everywhere cowered in fear that they would be the next victim. People point to stats that romance scams are on the rise and use that as a reason to avoid dating apps. It's true that romance scam victims lost a reported $547 million in 2021. What that stat ignores is the fact that all online scams were on the rise. The Federal Trade Commission (FTC) reports that $770 million in losses to scams can be attributed to contact that began on social media, making social media by far the biggest venue for internet fraud.

Why isn't there a TikTok Swindler movie on Netflix? Simply put, because it's not as sexy. Romance scams tap into all our greatest hopes and worst fears. And that is precisely what makes them so effective. *The Tinder Swindler* includes epic romance, intrigue, escape, and peril. We want to believe that love conquers all. When we are emotionally connected to the outcome, we can become illogical in our choices and overlook red flags. Let me spell out the most common techniques that scammers use so you can swipe as safely as possible.

Generic language: Is your heart going pitter-patter reading the flowery language and grand proclamations in the messages? The sender calls you beautiful and paints a picture of the life you two will have together in the future as soon as you can be together. Now, step back and reread the words as if they were meant for someone else—your mom, your sister, your best friend, your frenemy. Could the words your online lover said still make sense if they were delivered to someone else? Would it confirm their hopes and try to assuage their fears as well? Chances are you could be dealing with a scammer who copies and pastes messages to each of their online lovers, testing who will take the bait and then doubling down with other techniques to earn your trust . . . and your money.

Sketchy photos: If something looks iffy about their profile photos, your antennae should go up. If they seem too good to be true, they probably are. Look for photos that show people in uniform or who look like they are posed. How many doctors do you know that go around taking photos with their stethoscopes on or wear them to dates? Actually, one of the *Drew Barrymore Show* audience members who participated in an Ask Damona segment said a man she met online brought a stethoscope to the date. Needless to say, he was not actually a doctor.

Also, if the person has too few photos and refuses to send more, that's fishy. If there are any discrepancies between their photos and what they say in the written part of their profile, take note. Lastly, if their photos seem far away or grainy or if they don't seem like pictures of the same person, that is also a red flag.

Social proof: To get you to trust them, a scammer might construct social proof. This happens in *The Tinder Swindler* when he knows women would be looking him up on Instagram to corroborate his story. The movie and subsequent TV show *Catfish* started when Nev Schulman was contacted by a woman with a fake profile on Facebook. On the show, you see savvy catfish go so far as to build imaginary friends lists, even with people in their target's network, to appear more real and trustworthy to them.

My go-to secret weapon is not to search for a Facebook or even an Instagram profile. The real internet dating sleuths search on LinkedIn. If your successful businessman is under fifty-five and does not have a LinkedIn profile, either he's not that good of a businessman or he's not a businessman at all.

Taking you off the platform: This brings me to another key element of romance scams: trying to get you off of the dating platform. Being asked for your phone number so that the scammer can take you into the Texting Trap is now a dating right of passage. It indicates that you have gotten the rose and will be going on to the next episode. Be on alert, however, if, like in *The Tinder Swindler*, the person asks you to chat with them on WhatsApp.

WhatsApp is the most popular communication app for speaking with someone across borders, and it has enabled people throughout the world to connect freely from country to country. This convenient feature also makes it the preferred app for scammers of all kinds to communicate with you from any location in the world. Best news for them, the app is not tracking what they say to you and they can disrupt the communication flow between where they source their marks and where they close their transactions.

As soon as you leave the dating app, whether you go to the phone, an app, or a video chat platform, the dating app loses the ability to advocate for you, remove that person from the platform automatically, or gather evidence of what they've said to you for any legal purposes down the road.

For over a decade, moving off the app has signified unlocking a new level in the relationship. If you're texting with someone off the app, it gives the illusion that you're not being tempted by new matches on the app anymore. But we're in a new era of safety and security and many apps are responding by including tools like audio and video calling to keep you on the app for as long as possible.

You just have to have the confidence to hold to your boundaries when someone asks for your number and you have to explain that you prefer to keep chatting within the app. Allay their fears that it's a sign of disinterest.

It's only awkward if you make it awkward! Safety first.

Urgency: Another hallmark of digital romance scams is that there is always an urgency to the connection. The need to meet you right away. They want you to commit to being in a relationship within a week or two, even if you've never met. They had a sudden crisis and they need you to wire them money immediately or they will be _____ [insert crisis: stranded in a strange country, attacked by an angry mob, cut off by their phone carrier, unable to save their dying dog, unable to come see you].

Asking for money: We've arrived at the number one sign of the scammer: the request for money. It can come out of the blue and seem surprising after they painted a picture of having it all together. It often is presented as a condition for continuing your relationship. There is no reason why your online significant other should need money from you. Bottom line, dating apps can be terrifying, but in many ways they are actually safer than the way we used to date. I couldn't tell you the last name of any of the random men I met in dark downtown bars and summer house parties, but your dating app could identify the current location of the person who sent you a dick pic, so pick your dating risk poison.

Ultimately, you can mitigate much of your risk as long as you're following the basic safety precautions that most apps recommend:

1. Do a basic Google or social media search.
2. Meet your date in a public place that you're familiar with.
3. Share your location and identifying information about your date with a friend.
4. Agree to check in with your friend once you're home or set a time when they should contact you if they haven't received word.

And most of all, know that if you've never met your date in person, you're not in an actual relationship. The longer the relationship continues offline unverified, the more likely it is to be a scam or to end in disaster, or both.

CATFISH CASE STUDY: MISMATCHED

Prior to working with me, my client Mary had a date with a guy she met online. His profile had only two pictures. One was cute and the other was a group shot taken from far away. She was slightly suspicious, but they hit it off in messaging and later over the phone, so she agreed to meet up with him. When she arrived, she unknowingly stared right into the eyes of her date and then looked the other way. He introduced himself and her jaw dropped. He looked nothing like the photo he'd used on the app. They sat down for dinner and she couldn't shake the suspicion that this man was in no way the man whose picture she'd seen on the app.

Mary couldn't end the evening without asking him about the discrepancy. He hung his head in shame and admitted the first photo was of his friend. The group photo included him, but he'd intentionally used an unclear picture to make it more convincing. He wasn't a bad-looking guy, but his self-esteem was so low he didn't think he could attract women with his own photos, so he stole someone else's. She asked if anyone else had ever called him out on it. To Mary's surprise, he said no. Needless to say, she didn't go on another date with him. The biggest shame was that he might have had a chance with her if he'd just been honest in his profile from the start.

Before you meet up, if you're feeling suspicious, as mentioned before, it's a good idea to Google them. Look for photos associated with their name that seem mismatched with the ones you've already seen. Look for photos of them with someone else such as a spouse or girlfriend.

If you want to really get your Google Sleuth graduate degree, you can do a reverse image search in Google to see whether a photo they've posted is associated with any other names, photos, profiles, or conflicting information.

And regarding your own profile, it should go without saying even though more than half of daters admit to lying about something in their dating profile, don't do it. By now, you probably know how that story will end.

So many factors contribute to the mythical feeling of chemistry. The pursuit of this experience leaves so many daters chasing something that they may never find. I often wonder if we use chemistry as an excuse, a reason not to dive deeper inward and figure out what we really need and how to build a long-lasting connection. Chemistry is an easy out. As long as you can say you didn't feel the spark, you can walk away from any romance unscathed. You don't have to be vulnerable or introspective about what that spark is signifying to you and where you might actually need to change your approach or shift your beliefs.

That spark is familiarity. It's a feeling that you recognize or someone you know how to respond to. But that doesn't mean it's healthy or that they are the right person for you. True compatibility can't be determined by a spark. The road to deeper connection and understanding is through communication. There's no shortcut for truly getting to know who someone is, how they look at the world, what they value, and how their words and actions impact you.

The good news is we have more communication tools than ever before. If you know how to use them effectively and how to silence the chatter and interference, it's more possible than ever that you will make a meaningful connection, whether that person is across town or across the globe.

The Date phase is a crucial place for introspection and innovation. Many daters come to me disappointed that their dates do not clear the bar and bored over doing the same kinds of dates over and over again. The big aha comes when you recognize that you are cocreating the experience with the person sitting across from you. You must be an active participant and take personal responsibility for how the experience unfolds.

The Date phase is where you start to put together the thought work from The Mindset phase and the strategy from The Search phase and get into action. Science and history show us that it's not the visualization, it's not the planning, it's taking action that creates change. So, if you want to change your love life or relationship status, put the tools of The Date phase into practice. Your future partner awaits!

THE DATE ACTION STEPS

1. *Prepare.* Mentally, physically, and intellectually prepare for your dates so you can show up as your most authentic self.
2. *Be present.* Listening leads you to ask better questions, tell your story more effectively, and experience better dates.
3. *Curiosity > chemistry.* Stay in the moment and stay curious to identify how you truly feel on dates and who you can make a long-term connection with.
4. *Fight fair.* Conflict is inevitable, but you must learn how to repair after a rupture to make a relationship grow stronger.

part IV

the future

the soulmate myth

ONCE UPON A TIME, THERE WAS A VERY PATIENT PERSON. Their fairy godmother told them that a mythical being called a soulmate would come and find them one day and they would live happily ever after. Eventually, they started to ask, "After what?" After their entire life passed by? After they dismissed every possible partner because they were waiting for The One? When the spell wore off, they were just sitting there with a bunch of rats and pumpkins cursing their godmother's broken spell.

If I had a dime for every time someone told me they wanted to find their soulmate, I'd have about $81.20. It's not enough to retire on, so instead of hoping divine intervention would bring my clients success, I got curious about how this Soulmate Myth took root in the first place.

THE SOULMATE STORY

My grandmother passed away when I was twenty-four. Some families pass down material wealth to the next generation, but living in an immigrant family through the Great Depression made my grandma painfully frugal. She rocked reusable grocery bags before they were cool and would send me to three different stores clutching a handful of coupons just to save $1.95.

As her only granddaughter, after her passing I was given her jewelry box and the contents therein. Not surprisingly, the most precious item in it wouldn't go for seven bucks at a Goodwill. I was after something much more valuable among the unclaimed treasures she left behind: her many volumes of books, with detailed book club annotations scribbled alongside the text in her carefully crafted cursive. One of the volumes I treasured most was her five-book series on philosophy. That is when I first connected with Plato.

Thumbing through Plato's *The Republic*, I could see how my grandmother grappled with societal rules too. Handwritten notes like "women should be equal to men" nod to her experience of being relegated to two possible roles in her lifetime: teacher and mom. Her brilliance leaps off the page in those slim margins, where she contemplated her own truth.

From *The Republic* and my grandmother's captivating notes I was led to discover Plato's *Symposium*, which many scholars believe is the first recorded mention of the concept of soulmates. I can almost imagine her thoughts appearing in the margins when I read it.

A symposium was the aristocratic entertainment of the day that involved a banquet, heavy drinking, and lots of musing about life. Plato's *Symposium* imagines one such gathering with a series of speeches given in praise of Eros, the god of love and desire, by well-known figures of the time, including the famous playwright Aristophanes and Plato's real-life mentor, Socrates.

Aristophanes's speech proposes the idea that originally there were three types of human: male-male, female-female, and a third type made of both genders. They were figures with four hands, four feet, and were completely round because they were offspring of the sun, the earth, and the moon. These creatures grew so powerful that the gods were worried they'd attack and overthrow them, so Zeus hatched a plan. He suggested they cut the creatures in half and reshape them into what we now know as the human form, which left them on an epic, never-ending quest for their other halves. "They were ready to die of hunger in one another's arms," Aristophanes's speech proclaims. He continues, "Love is the desire of the whole and the pursuit of the whole is called love."

Philosophers believe that the work was intended to be satire, but people took Plato's clever idea of finding our "other half" and ran with it. The intent got stripped away, the myth was created, and the soulmate story spread like wildfire throughout our culture. We are basically living through the meme-ification of Plato's *Symposium*.

Here's the issue with the Soulmate Myth: if your sad, lonely, half-souled carcass is just dragging around the earth in search of its one and only cosmic connection, it absolves you of the need to do anything to bring your other half to you. You're just playing out your destiny, and either it's meant to be that you will be reunited or it's simply not in the cards for you. This was pretty and poetic for ancient Greek literature, but let's be real: How could you be predestined to meet one person on a planet with eight billion people?

Yet still, the soulmate strategy prevails for the majority of daters. When the matching question "Is a soulmate worth waiting for?" popped up on OkCupid, 90 percent of respondents said yes. I've seen similar attitudes among my listeners, clients, and participants in other studies I've read. This means that the majority of people believe that there is one person out there for them. One person who is meant to fit together with them like a puzzle piece. One needle in a global-sized haystack designed to fulfill all of your needs and be your mirror image, ensuring a frictionless relationship. And you're supposed to just sit around and wait to find each other so you can become whole again.

Plato's *Symposium* is also the birthplace of the term *platonic love*. Which, of course, we've also misconstrued over the years. He regarded the highest love as the love of the truth. Plato proposed through Socrates's speech in *Symposium* that our deepest relationships would teach us about beauty in the world, lead us to be more virtuous, and give us knowledge about the true meaning of life. He saw love like a ladder that began with physical attraction but evolved into something deeper: soul discovery and our ultimate truth. Therefore, platonic love is not just nonromantic love but actually love that transcends a sexual connection into a deeper understanding of ourselves and our place in the world.

As romantic as having a soulmate sounds, pursuing that ideal keeps you constantly in a scarcity mindset. If there is only one person who could match with you, your choices will always feel limited, and even if you meet someone wonderful, there will always be a voice in your mind asking, "Is this person actually The One?" Trading up to an abundance mindset will increase your chances of finding and keeping love. Better still, it will lead you to a deeper understanding of your truth.

If you're in a relationship with someone great but the nagging question of whether this person is your *soulmate* occupies your mind, you may never be fully committed to working through the challenging times with this person. Will you be motivated to get to the deeper relationship waiting for you on the other side of perfection?

When I was on the TV series *#BlackLove*, someone asked my cohost, Jack A. Daniels, and me if we believed in soulmates. Both being happily married and working in the relationship profession (he's a psychotherapist), we shocked the room when I immediately blurted out no and he instantly said yes. Most people are surprised to find that I don't believe in soulmates because my husband and I have been together so long. Fun fact: Mr. Hoffman doesn't believe in soulmates either.

We believe that there are many possible matches out there for you, but you choose to make someone your soulmate every day you choose to keep learning and growing into your relationship. My husband is an incredible match for me and we have grown to be even more compatible in the time we've been together, but it wasn't obvious to me from the start.

Did I feel butterflies immediately? Not really, but I thought he was cute, a little preppy for my style, but cute. Did I know his entire life story? No, but I was intrigued by his depth and intellect and I wanted to know more. Did I know we were meant to be? No way, although my roommate did tell me he was The One after meeting him on date three—although I'm still not sure how she figured it out long before I did; maybe a lucky guess.

That's because it took me years to determine whether we fit along the Four Pillars: Goals, Values, Communication, and Trust. From the beginning, we had shared values and goals for the future. Next, we discovered we had very different yet compatible communication styles. However, as a child of divorce, trust didn't come naturally to me. We both had to earn that pillar.

The longer we dated, the clearer it became that our Four Pillars were aligned. When he proposed to me, the only possible answer was, "Of course." He leads me to my truth. It is both platonic and romantic love.

YOUR DATING DESTINY

We spend a lot of our time on this planet musing about what is meant to be. We cling to potential and create false narratives based on momentary feelings because the exciting unknown is always more compelling than the mundane moment we are in.

> Dear Damona,
> I think I found The One in my closest friend's younger brother. I had a feeling about him years ago and then met him again recently and there was a spark that I hadn't felt before with anyone. He texted me a few times, but I didn't expect much. I think he felt the spark, too, but there hasn't been a dialogue about it. Am I on the right track or am I destined to be alone forever?

We love to live in extremes because it makes us feel alive. Yet, there's a lot of open space in between *the right track* and *alone forever* and I don't see destiny anywhere in there. The reality right now seems to be that this letter writer is in a textationship, at best. Designing our destiny based on a spark or a hunch can be enticing for a time, but at some point we have to look at the facts.

I'd say to this person that until you actually spend more time together or confirm whether he feels the same way, you're neither destined to be alone forever nor on the right track. You're simply fantasizing about one possible outcome. The idea of destiny keeps many psychics employed and many singles on a never-ending quest to find their one true person. Our addiction to storytelling drives us to know the ending to our love story and prevents us from living in the present and growing with a relationship day by day.

SOCIAL MEDIA PSYCHOLOGY

We can't talk about planning for the future without nodding to attachment styles and love languages. They are the two most prominent tools for determining your relationship future, according to dating blogs, social media, and lifestyle magazines. Everyone loves a "which one am I?" quiz. I am in favor of any framework that helps you understand your relationship conditioning and gives you the tools to communicate with your partner more effectively, but these two modalities are often misunderstood in popular culture.

Dr. Gary Chapman developed the Five Love Languages on the basis of the challenges he saw married couples in his

Christian ministry confronting. In 1992, his book *The Five Love Languages* was published to some success, but in recent years, as BuzzFeed quiz culture took root, its popularity skyrocketed and the public's understanding of the love languages tool moved away from its origin.

In case you've been living under a rock for thirty years or, like my husband, you don't have a social media account, the Five Love Languages are quality time, physical touch, gifts, words of affirmation, and acts of service.

First, the original teachings within *The Five Love Languages* emphasize learning your partner's love language and meeting them there. But it's no fun to take a quiz about your partner; we need to know about ourselves, right? Today people tout their love language in casual conversation, on first dates, and even in dating profiles as a shortcut to attracting someone who "gets" them.

Yet as with most ideas from the 1990s, it may be time for a rewrite. The Five Love Languages are based on relationship issues that commonly come up for traditional, heterosexual, classic-gender-role relationships. When this theory was developed, most of the women studied were responsible for caring for the house while men worked outside the home. Acts of service today has come to signify that you like having little things done for you (without having to ask). Originally, however, it meant men doing additional things around the house that weren't technically part of their household responsibilities to unburden their wives and make them feel appreciated.

In no way am I diminishing the validity of the Five Love Languages, but it's important to understand how the methodology was developed and determine which parts suit your particular lifestyle and relationship roles. One big takeaway is to also approach love languages with the understanding that this framework was designed to help *you* be a better partner who knows and speaks your partner's love language rather than as a matchmaking shortcut to attract someone who can easily plug into your life.

ATTACHMENT STYLES

I'm not an expert in attachment theory, but I believe that it's a great framework when used by a qualified professional and a big old mess when used to self-diagnose or explain away unsavory behaviors in a partner.

Similar to the Five Love Languages, there's a pervasive trend to label one's attachment style after completing the rigorous self-study of watching an Instagram reel. According to the research of John Bowlby and Mary Ainsworth in the 1950s and 1960s, attachment styles are imprinted on you and based on your relationship with your primary caregiver (specifically, your mother in the original study).

The primary attachment styles are anxious, avoidant, and secure. There are also variations and subcategories, but for the purpose of simplicity we'll stick with the big three. In the simplest terms, if you have anxious attachment, you tend to rush into partnership quickly. The idea of being alone is frightening to you, and when one relationship ends, you're ready to rush into the next one right away. If you have avoidant attachment, you experience the opposite. You want closeness, but when it happens, you feel suffocated and want to retreat. You might even self-sabotage situations to keep yourself from getting too close. Finally, secure attachment is basically the style of that magical population of people who avoid relationship drama.

Contrary to popular social media belief, we are not permanently broken if we tend toward anxious or avoidant attachment. We are constantly playing out our biological conditioning in relationships, and in the best of circumstances, we can use these guidelines to inform us and help us grow. In my practice, I've seen a much wider variety of attachment styles than the basic three, and I've observed that different people bring out different sides of us. Today there are varied kinds of family structures, and psychologists have come to embrace that you can have many attachment figures beyond just your mother. I believe that we'll come to understand a more expansive view of attachment theory with more research. In the meantime, it's just one data point.

You are not stuck with the attachment cards you've been dealt, and even if you have had an avoidant attachment style in the past, you can feel secure in a relationship if you and your partner share a relationship growth mindset.

RELATIONSHIP GROWTH MINDSET

I'm not telling you to settle. I'm telling you that you're going to meet someone pretty great. You'll be attracted to them, they'll have a lot of qualities you're looking for, they'll share your values and maybe even your goals, too. But they'll be a terrible dresser or they'll chew their food loudly or their sense of humor will be a little corny. Then you'll have a choice. Walk away or adopt a relationship growth mindset.

A relationship growth mindset means you can change together and learn from one another. Perhaps they will learn to chew more quietly or will develop a more sophisticated sense of humor. Or not. More likely, you will learn that how they chew their food has nothing to do with who they are as a person or how willing they are to grow into an expansive shared life with you.

Many people miss potential soulmates because they don't know what it's supposed to feel like when they meet The One. We tend to be so focused on the outcome of having a soulmate that we don't realize there's a soulmate sitting right in front of us in the present moment. Rather than thinking ahead into the distant future, when I met my husband, I focused on our day-to-day experience. Each day, we chose to be together another day. Days turned into weeks and weeks turned into years and nearly twenty years later, here we are still choosing.

That element of choice is vitally important. When you are looking for the ideal soulmate, many times you forget just how many choices you get to make in your search for lasting partnership. Having choice is a privilege, but if you don't use the ability to choose, you lose it.

When you've exhausted all of the myths, you're left with the truth and that truth will lead you to the ultimate foundation of any great long-term relationship: trust.

chapter 12

the trust pillar

I INVITE YOU TO REPLACE THE SOULMATE MYTH THAT HAS BEEN holding us back from happiness with reality. Your soulmate isn't magic. The pillar that determines your relationship future is trust, and there's no shortcut to it. Trust is built in small moments, micro-decisions, and actions that align with words.

TRUST BEGINS WITH SURRENDERING

How do you build trust with a partner? At its core, trust is about truth. However, it's not something you can will into existence with force. It's helpful to see conflicts or worries as opportunities rather than roadblocks. If you feel triggered by something your partner does, can you slow down and get curious about why your first instinct is to react? Is this a pattern that existed before your partner? Instead of a remnant of the past, could this be a signpost pointing toward your future? Can you respond with that awareness rather than react? Would it potentially lead to a different outcome if you stepped into the opportunity to choose a different response? It's difficult to build trust if we have residual feelings that are being transferred to a new partner and our mind runs the same plays from before.

> Dear Damona,
> My partner and I both dealt with infidelity in past relationships. I want to be able to trust him, but I don't know how to start fresh after what happened to me before. He's never done anything to make me think he would be unfaithful, but still, I worry about it all the time.

Trust is something you have to surrender into and that act of surrendering is not something most of us have practice with. We're so used to always doing or fixing that it's hard to simply allow. Furthermore, it's hard to see the truth if it's not in alignment with the stories we've been telling ourselves.

The first step to building trust is to listen between the lines. Most people speak their truth, usually early on in the relationship. Trust means being able to actually hear your partner without pushing for your desired outcome. When your partner says something that makes you question their motives or your relationship future, instead of getting defensive or controlling, get curious. Ask follow-up questions that confirm you heard what they said and allow them to reveal more of themselves, like,

"When you said this, what did you mean?" or "Can you tell me more about that?" Then get quiet. As you learned in prior chapters, real understanding is bridged through listening. Yet in conversation most of us aren't listening but are waiting for our turn to speak. That's why most people you meet at a cocktail party have already forgotten your name before the first round of hors d'oeuvres comes out.

The next step in building trust is alignment. How do your partner's words and actions align with one another? Does your partner do what they say they're going to do? Do they show up when they promise you they'll be there? Or do their actions create confusion for you? Trust happens when we see consistency from our partner and their words and actions match up.

The key final ingredient for trust is time. We often receive a gut feeling about whether we can trust someone. That intuition, as you've seen already, is a powerful guide, but it is not trust. To build trust in a relationship, you have to see which feelings appear in repetition. Do you consistently feel safe with them? Do they always show up for you, not just for a month or two or when it's convenient for them?

Trust is so sweet when you achieve it. It allows you to relax and feel safe. We are always on the push in our lives, but the building blocks of trust can lead you to a place where you don't have to work so hard. You can just surrender and allow love to unfold, breaking the patterns of the past.

Plato said love is about the pursuit of truth. The truth cannot be bent to your will or the will of your partner. Eventually, truth in relationships will be revealed. The question is how much time, effort, and pain will you sacrifice to reach it?

> *Dear Damona,*
>
> *How do you know if a relationship is worth fighting for? I've caught my boyfriend in lies several times in the past. Every time, he says he's going to stop lying, that he's trying, but I'm losing hope that he'll ever change. I'm not even sure I know what it looks like to be able to trust someone. My dad was the same way and always lying to my mom and I feel like I'm repeating the same cycle. I really love my boyfriend, but I don't know how much more of this I can take.*

If you come from a family where you did not learn how to trust or feel safe in a relationship, it is hard to recognize the warning signs that someone is going to send you right into acting out an old script. In the case of this letter writer, that script isn't even theirs—it's a script that their parents wrote and that they witnessed play out so many times they started to think that was how the story should go.

Even thinking of a relationship as something to "fight for" puts us in an offensive stance that places the relationship outside of ourselves instead of centering us within it. You and your partner are the relationship, you're not battling against it. Still, I understand that it's exhausting to set up boundaries and have them constantly bowled over.

Can someone change? Of course! But the drive to change has to be greater than the consequence of not changing. Two factors motivate people's behavior: moving toward pleasure and moving away from pain. For your partner's behavior and, therefore, your relationship to change, the reward or the consequence must be stronger. How long are you going to carry the pain someone else is causing you? Who has the stronger motivation to change? Is the pain caused by your partner's lying great enough, or is it pushing away so much pleasure, that they are inspired to change? Or are you in so much pain that your partner's lying overshadows the pleasure you get from the relationship? Until one of those forces becomes stronger, a relationship can stay in limbo indefinitely. It takes a firm boundary or decisive action to move out of this cycle. You can't surrender into trust if trust has not been built. It all comes back to our samskaras, those stories we've inherited, written for ourselves, and continue to play out until you make a bold move to change the story.

ONLINE DISINHIBITION

Before we can get to building trust with a long-term partner, we have to address the lack of trust that most singles have in dating. If you can't even trust that a date will keep their word and not stand you up or cancel plans at the last minute, how can you trust that the next time might be different?

Even Drew Barrymore has shared with me and her audience that someone she met on a dating app stood her up for a date. This left her, understandably, nervous about dating apps and the integrity of men who express interest in her. Though the exact experience may be different, you don't have to be a celebrity to know this feeling.

Ultimately, what we are facing is a breakdown in empathy for daters. I believe this is driven largely by the online disinhibition effect. Researchers coined this term to describe why people say things online that they wouldn't have the confidence to say to someone face-to-face. Usually, this is used in connection with your unfriendly neighborhood Twitter troll. However, I also find that many daters treat people they haven't yet bonded with as disposable.

Although we cannot control how others treat us, we can control how we show up in dating. We can control whether we let those who insensitively ghosted us impact our enthusiasm for dating as a whole. We can also control whether we treat the next person with kindness, respect, and empathy. An unpopular opinion is coming your way: People will complain about getting ghosted while at the same time ghosting others they don't see as viable matches. Eventually, as more people clean up their side of the emotional balance street, the dating neighborhood could turn around. But it won't change just by complaining about it or moving away from online dating.

As we get past those first few dates, we start to explore the interesting territory of building trust and connection. Using my Three Date Rule, let curiosity drive the first three dates. Then, somewhere between three dates and three months, you usually will begin to contemplate or move into that next stage of dating: becoming a couple. With trust, you can turn couplehood into the fourth and final stage: commitment.

We can't be in too much of a hurry to get to that final stage, though. Many people chase the label of "couple" but want to shortcut the journey to get there. We want the bikini body, but we'd love to skip the part about all those sit-ups. But you don't want to skip relationship steps because those trials and tribulations will tell you what your relationship is truly made of.

FOLLOW-THROUGH

Dates are often made or broken not by what happens on the date but by what happens afterward. If you're caught up in the Soulmate Myth, you might be thinking that if it's meant to be, it'll be, no matter what. Not only is that false, but it also gives away all your power. You have more control over the outcome of your love life than you've been led to believe. Developing follow-through enables you to do what is in your control to steer where the relationship is headed. It makes you an active participant in your future and someone who takes responsibility for your actions. Without knowing how to properly follow through, you could be doing everything else in your dating process right but find yourself continually stuck in this phase, unable to progress your relationships to the next level. If we rely on the Soulmate Myth, we think it'll just work out if it's meant to be, and we miss the chance to play an active role in shaping the trajectory of our lives.

First, we have to pay attention to how we feel with someone on a date and what we would like to have happen. At the end of every *Washington Post* Date Lab interview, the daters are asked to rate the date on a scale of 1 to 5. Then they must give me an update before the piece goes to print. I'm crushed every time people report having a date that is a 4 or 4.5 out of 5, then tell me that they had no further contact.

One date in particular, the couple made an incredible connection. Both of them even noted in their interviews that they were shocked that we had found such an ideal match. They had a surprising amount in common: they studied a similar topic in school, enjoyed the same hobbies, listened to similar music, and genuinely had a fantastic conversation. At the end of the date, though, the mixed messages they sent left them in limbo.

In our post-date interview, the woman told me she tore off a piece of paper, scribbled down her number, and said, "There's lots to do around H Street where I live." However, the man recounted the same exchange as: "If you're on H Street and looking to hang out, here's my number." He assumed this meant that she was not looking for romance. Whether there was potential here for a real relationship or not, we will never know because the date ended in confusion and the follow-through plan was unclear.

We freeze or flee when faced with the possibility that someone might turn us down when we express our interest in them. When no one is willing to risk expressing their interest, you are left in relationship no-man's-land. What are we really afraid of? Especially when we're talking about a person we've just met online or had a date or two with, how high is that risk, really? In certain situations, the stakes of sharing your feelings are higher, such as if you work together or have friends in common. But in most casual dating, the worst outcome is possibly running into this person in the grocery store. Incidentally, this happened to me a few years ago and I can assure you that you can just intently stare at the cereal boxes and pretend that you don't even see one another. The awkward moment will pass and you'll be fine.

The issue is, we tend to look at each possible connection as having equal stakes or intensity, but most of these dating decisions are not life or death. We guard our heart from looking foolish or feeling overexposed, when the reality is that the biggest pain you will suffer is that of an unrealized relationship—a love that will never be because you were afraid to be vulnerable and express interest in the other person.

An attitude of apathy pervades dating today. Because of the increased speed of courtship, we suffer so many more micro-disappointments that we are afraid to risk at all. I meet this apathy with empathy and authenticity. Until you express your true feelings and lean into your curiosity, the relationship you desire will always appear to be on the other side of the glass.

FOLLOW-THROUGH POP QUIZ

Let's imagine for a moment that you make it through a great first date. The follow-through actually begins before you've even left one another. How do you end it? Do you:

A. Tell them you'll see them around.
B. Give them a handshake and say it was nice to meet them.
C. Let them know you'd love to see them again.
D. Just go for it and start making out.

Of course, you're a grown-up and you can choose to do any one of these options, but if you're looking for the relationship to continue, I'm a fan of option C. When I was doing my dating coaching certification program, I was taught to have my clients take a more neutral approach, but I can't help it, I'm a fiery Sagittarius. I actually encourage my clients to be more forthcoming with their feelings, whether they're interested or don't feel like it's a match.

You become emotionally tethered to the people you meet, and keeping things in limbo only generates additional stress for you. Many psychologists are studying the impact of this new phenomenon of undefined relationships and the early data isn't looking good for our health, in spite of terms like "situationship" seeing massive growth in mentions on dating app profiles in the last year.

If you know that you're not interested, I find that most people would rather just hear it than have you slink away into the night or give them false hope that you'll go out again. Keeping that loop open subjects you to continual check-in texts that you don't want. It's possible that the person might not take no for an answer and could still try to change your mind, but statistically speaking, most people appreciate clarity.

I have heard from some clients that they don't feel physically safe turning someone down face-to-face. Obviously, if you're not in a safe space with someone you trust, make the choice that is going to be the safest option for you. But then I ask, Who are these people you're hanging out with? If you get to the point of feeling unsafe with your dates, please revisit your screening process and tighten up your filter.

Conversely, if you are really excited to see someone again, what would happen if you expressed your enthusiasm at the end of the date? When I write for Date Lab, I'm not coaching, I'm reporting, so I can't get involved in the outcome. Yet after interviewing two daters and hearing about the amazing connection and conversation they shared, it takes everything in me not to tell them that they should just pick up the phone and ask the other person out again.

I've never seen a client be disappointed when they've expressed interest in someone in the first few dates. But I see plenty of rumination about what could have happened if they were more open. We suffocate on the what-ifs. We underestimate the scarcity of connection.

Ultimately, you will have a physical attraction to only a few people who share your values and goals and who you plain old enjoy spending time with. We think that a big lightbulb is supposed to go off telling us that this person is The One. In the meantime, we let a lot of *ones* slip through our fingers.

MOMENTUM

After you cross the threshold into dates two, three, four, and beyond, the momentum takes over. Once you step on the relationship escalator by continuing to date one person, the escalator will push you on to the next phase of dating and the unique questions and challenges therein.

Make sure that the speed of your escalator is not too fast, or you will miss the most exciting parts. The first six weeks of dating are foundational and set the tone of the relationship going forward. It's actually one of my favorite times to coach clients through because I know that this moment in this relationship will only happen once.

The strangest thing about this escalator is that there is no actual destination. Some think that their stop is marriage, but that is just the starting point of another escalator. Relationships are more like the Willy Wonka elevator that can take you and your partner to any possible destination. Although dating goals are important, try to set aside expectations around timelines. After the first six weeks of slow love, each relationship settles into its own pacing.

chapter 13

F soulmates, fix your future

IN MY PROGRAM, WE GET VERY TACTICAL AND TECHNICAL about dating apps, conversation techniques, and flirting. This prepares us to step into more speculative skills that are also vital in dating, the most important of which is intuition.

We are groomed to believe that if we don't have tangible evidence for something, it's not real. We are taught that all of our thinking takes place inside of our brain. However, compelling research shows we can take in information from outside of our thinking mind. Beyond the signals that our body delivers from our gut, we get information from other parts of our bodies, too. Tapping into how fast our heart is beating or how cold our hands and feet feel can guide us in our decisions. You're hearing your body speak to you all the time, but you have to correlate those signals with choosing the right outcome in order to trust your gut.

We access our intuition first by looking for patterns. Let's try an exercise that helps your body recognize its warning signs.

EXERCISE: PAST RELATIONSHIP SIGNALS

Think about a positive past relationship. How did it feel to be with that person? Do you remember things they would specifically say or do that gave you that warm feeling? Where in your body did you feel that? Was it a warmth in your chest? A tingle in your spine? What do you feel now when you think about them?

Now what about when you were in a bad relationship? What do you remember feeling with that person? Where did it show up in your body? How did that relationship influence you internally? Do you recall having mental or physical health changes during the time you were together?

You can also try this exercise thinking about family members, coworkers, and friends. How does their presence affect you? Where in your body do you feel a sensation when you're talking to or about them? Does your throat feel tight? Are your fingers cold? Does your body feel flushed all over?

Now focus on one of those sensations or thoughts. Think about other times when you felt those feelings in other situations or with other people. Is there any correlation between the two? Did the relationships follow a similar pattern? Or did they have a similar outcome?

Your body's intuition can recognize a similarity that may be invisible to you on a conscious level. Researchers have found that in response to new stimuli or people, physical changes occur in our bodies first, before our emotional and cognitive brain can process them. Your body often sends a warning signal about how the relationship is impacting you before your brain tells you what to do. Pay attention to those physiological changes in your body as you're dating. Ask yourself, "When have I felt this before? And what was the outcome of that relationship or situation?"

Interoception is the scientific term for the perception of sensations inside your body and psychologists are rapidly incorporating this long-overlooked aspect of emotional regulation into their work. I see interoception as the first step in developing a deeper level of intuition. Tuning in to your internal compass helps you read your body's signals more clearly and enables you to trust what your intuition is telling you. As Dr. Drew Pinsky said, "The body is a perfect instrument." Exercises like this one help you tune yours.

CASE STUDY: QUIETING THE ANXIOUS MIND

My client Mandy was admittedly an anxious person. She came to me a few months after being dumped by a man she thought she was going to marry. Mandy was determined to meet her person in a hurry. She jumped into online dating with both feet, and within a couple weeks she already had half a dozen dates lining up. Very quickly, she made a deeper connection with one of her dates but had a hard time trusting her gut, especially because it was all happening so fast.

When I asked her how she felt, she would use statements like, "I think he's a good guy" or "I think the problem is that I'm comparing him to my ex." In our sessions, I encouraged her every time she caught herself saying *think* to instead pause and say *feel*. This allowed her to access full-body listening when she was on dates with him and quiet that bossy, anxious mind that was always telling her what to do.

Additionally, I encouraged her to develop a daily meditation practice. It's impossible to embrace your intuition if you're constantly processing racing thoughts and thinking through what-if scenarios. Meditation, whether you do two minutes or two hours a day, helps create space in between the racing thoughts to bring you clarity.

Eventually, she was able to find clarity about one of the men she'd met, who was exactly what she was looking for. She's now in what she says is the healthiest relationship of her life. After they moved in together, she continued to use meditation as a tool to bring her anxiety down in her relationship and has even brought meditation into his life as well. The couple who meditates together is less anxious together.

BEGINNING WITH MINDFULNESS

Slow love, which we talked about in the Introduction, is our best tool for developing trust, and meditation and mindfulness can help us keep calm and carry on with getting to know someone. A great place to begin with meditation and mindfulness is simply to get in touch with your five senses whenever you feel emotionally heightened or when you want to reset yourself—even on a date. When you notice your nervous system being hijacked by anxiety, pause and internally complete the phrases: I hear _____, I see _____, I smell _____, I taste _____, I feel _____. Take note that *I think* is not in that list.

Anxiety commonly presents itself when we are ruminating on the past or projecting into the future. A mindfulness practice helps you stay grounded in the present as you go through the ups and downs of dating and forming a new relationship.

Anxiety also bubbles up when there is dissonance. When our expectations or hopes are not aligned with reality or when our goals seem to compete with those of people around us, we start to second-guess our feelings. It's easy to get caught up in what others' beliefs or relationship expectations are for you, but no one else except you and potential partners have the answers to your relationship future. Meditation and mindfulness help you quiet external voices and recenter on your own needs and desires.

DATE RATE

My *Dates & Mates* listeners are busy bees and they demand relationship timelines. *How often should we see each other? How long do we have to date before we can have the DTR (Define the Relationship) talk?* they often ask.

Sorry to say, this isn't Disneyland, you can't look at the wait times before you enter the queue. You're just going to have to take the ride. Plus, I would argue that the wait is actually the most interesting part because it's where all the discovery lies. If you reframe your thinking, instead, to see the discovery phase as information gathering rather than an icky awkwardness that you can't wait to escape, you will spend less time clock watching and more time living your love life.

That said, I have to again wave the cue card for slow love. As much as you would like to jump in with both feet at the beginning, try to space out your interactions with your date, in that first month especially. Modern daters fear that if you like someone and you don't lock it down right away, a meant-to-be relationship will elude you. This couldn't be further from the truth. If you give the person space in the first few weeks and they keep coming back, you know that you have the stuff that long-term-relationship potential is made of.

Aim for a "date rate" of no more than two dates per week in the first month of dating. This allows you distance between dates to figure out how you feel about the other person and to see how they show up for you.

Seeing someone daily right out of the gate actually changes your body's physiology. When we are in proximity to someone we care about, our body releases oxytocin. This is known as the "love hormone" because it is released when we are in love or when kindness is expressed between two people. The more time you spend with someone, whether romantic or platonic, merely relating to them in a positive way makes you feel bonded to them, and then more oxytocin flows. This is why you can get emotionally hooked early in the relationship and may blow through red flags or warning signs.

GET TO THE PART ABOUT THE SEX

We can't talk about oxytocin and timelines without talking about sex. One of the most common questions I receive is: How long should I wait to have sex?

I'm a sex-positive dating coach, and I never shame anyone for choosing to have sex on the first date or skipping the first date altogether and going right to their place. I can't tell you exactly what sex with someone you're dating means to that specific person, but I can tell you what is happening in your body and what statistically happens for my clients depending on when they have sex with their dates.

When you have sex with someone, oxytocin is released and, particularly for women, you can begin to feel bonded to them, whether you like it or not. Once you have sex, you can't get back that magical "will they or won't they" energy and the anticipation that you feel before the first time you do the deed. There's a massive exchange of energy during sex, and after you've been intimate, sex usually becomes the default unless you make a concerted effort to slow down and reset the relationship.

Sex can be complicated. There are physical and emotional ramifications, and, especially in light of the current restrictions on abortion and increasingly limited access to contraceptives and reproductive care, dealing with potential outcomes can be awkward. Here's the bottom line: you probably shouldn't have sex with someone until you feel comfortable enough to have a conversation about those possible complications. I know, how sexy, right? For most of my clients, this falls somewhere between three and ten dates. I'm in no way saying that if you have sex on the first date it will never last, but I can tell you that to the best of my knowledge, none of my clients is still with someone they slept with the first night. So, if you want it to last, what is the rush if you have your entire lives together ahead of you? And ten dates is only about six to eight weeks if you're seeing each other once or twice a week. I've had items in my refrigerator longer than that.

Researchers note that oxytocin is also the key hormone in boosting trust, yet we don't want that Trust Pillar to be a mirage. And the presence of oxytocin in your system does not necessarily mean that the other person is experiencing the same feelings.

Does it mean that you're exclusive once you've had sex? Definitely not. Sex means different things to different people, and making assumptions about what your date or potential partner is thinking or feeling is the fastest road to disappointment. Make sure you both are clear on your expectations before you cross that threshold, including whether or not you're sleeping with other people.

> Dear Damona,
> I've had one date with this girl and the date went really well and I just matched with someone else who I would like to get to know. Should I date more than one person at the same time? Would it get confusing? What's your advice around dating multiple people at the beginning and later down the road?

I encourage you to date multiple people at once. Putting your expectations into one match gives away too much of your power and freedom. The prevailing assumption is you are not exclusive with someone until proven otherwise, so the likelihood of them going on other dates is high. Even if you had a great date or two, there's no reason to force commitment too early, before you've had a chance to see whether that person can be trusted with your heart.

Eventually, you're going to have to have "The Talk." I promise it's not as scary as it seems in your mind right now. Here's a 1-2-3 script you can follow:

1. **Start with a personal share:** *I always have so much fun when I'm with you.*
2. **Reveal your intention:** *I'm going to take my profile down.*
3. **Open up to their response:** *What are your thoughts or feelings about that?*

There are many variations of the script and you can always turn up the intensity in your personal shares or intentions, but the important thing is that you end with a pause and *listen*.

This conversation can be so anxiety producing because we have an investment in a particular outcome—we want them to like us back. This causes us to try to overtalk the other person or push them toward a yes instead of really listening to what comes back.

I'll admit, the DTR conversation didn't go great the first time my husband and I had it. We had been dating for about eight weeks and I attended his birthday party without clarity on how I was supposed to introduce myself. Clearly, he was in the same boat, because he simply said to his friends, "This is Damona." The tell was in their reactions. They all responded with an intrigued, "Ohhhh." It was obvious they had heard of me, but no label accompanied my name.

After the party, I asked myself, "Do I want to be his girl-friend?" Even though the conversation hadn't happened before that event, I was clear that exclusivity was what I wanted and that we seemed to be headed in that direction. So, the next time we were on a date, walking side by side, I popped the question.

Difficult conversations can actually be eased if you engage in them when you're moving. First, walking gets your heart rate up and boosts your endorphins. Researchers report that when you think while in motion, you make better decisions. Next, being positioned side by side gives a feeling of closeness without the awkwardness of direct eye contact.

Even though I set the stage and teed the conversation up perfectly, when I actually asked the question, I was met with some hemming, hawing, and general uncertainty. I questioned if what I was feeling was real. On the basis of his friends' reaction and how he related to me at the party, I assumed that this conversation was a foregone conclusion. I was wrong.

He needed some time to think about it; he wasn't sure. He loved spending time with me, but he didn't know whether he wanted to be exclusive yet. I was spinning inside, but I kept my cool. "Okay," I told him. "Take your time and let me know." We went about our date that evening, but there was a giant elephant in the room.

After that, our relationship was back to business as usual. I didn't bring up the conversation again. I didn't try to plead my case again. I just waited, knowing that I couldn't press him. If he wasn't interested in being exclusive, he would at least know what I wanted and I'd know where he stood.

A few days later, he asked me to officially be his girlfriend. I asked why he had so much hesitation before and such clarity now. Apparently, he had been planning to ask me if he could introduce me at the party as his girlfriend, but the right moment never presented itself, and then when I brought it up, he was caught off guard. He'd also had a vision in his mind for how the conversation would play out, and what might have seemed like a rejection to me was actually his mind adjusting to a change in the story he was telling himself. If I'd overreacted or pushed him away after that conversation, I could have unraveled my dream relationship. We forget that our dates and partners are also grappling with their own myths and stories too.

This is why it's important to stay in curiosity, even beyond the initial dates. I didn't get overly attached to the outcome I wanted. I allowed enough space for both of us to come together on our own terms and in our own time.

MOVING IN TOGETHER

Norms around cohabitation have shifted more in the last few decades than almost any other element of dating or relationships. In the 1950s, cohabitation before marriage was essentially non-existent. That number began to rise in the mid-1960s, and today nearly 70 percent of adults have lived with a partner sometime in their life, prior to marriage.

On the TV series *A Question of Love*, I counseled three couples who were moving in together for a thirty-day experiment, and in that time, I found that the couples who asked the tough questions before moving in together were the ones who remained together after the experiment. Moving in together greatly ups the stakes in a relationship, but knowing that the vast majority of daters look at this as a vital relationship milestone, I had developed a framework of questions to ask before taking this step to fortify the foundation of the relationship. The three questions are simple, but their answers can be complex: why, how, and when.

Why: Ask yourself and your partner, Why are we moving in together? Is it to save rent? Is it a step forward in the relationship? Is it simply more geographically convenient? Or is it a promise of a future together? You must first make sure you and your partner are on the same page about what living together means, and asking this question aloud rather than making assumptions is clarifying.

How: Once you know you're both working toward the same relationship goals, you have to get into the logistics. In my practice, I've seen that it's universally better to move into a new place together so both parties can create the space individually and as a couple; however, that is not always feasible. Get clear on which space makes the most sense for both of you, how you're going to split the bills, divvy up household responsibilities, and handle other logistics before you put your name on the lease.

When: This question is not just about when you're going to take this step but also about when you're going to check in again. Many couples get into cohabitation situations where they feel stuck because they never committed to reevaluating the arrangement or devised an exit strategy in advance. Although this is not the most romantic part of the cohabitation conversation, it's a crucial one.

Also remember with this, and most tips in this book, just because something is the norm doesn't mean that you have to go along with it. On an episode of *The Drew Barrymore Show*, I fielded this question from the audience:

> *Dear Damona,*
> *What if I don't want to live with a partner? Should I put that in my dating profile?*

I reminded this audience member not to create a problem before she had one. Putting your desire to live alone in your profile makes a lot of assumptions about yourself and the person you're hoping to meet. You might have certain beliefs about what cohabitation means that dissolve once you meet someone you love. Also, if you've been living alone for a long period of time, it can feel uncomfortable to think of giving up some of your space and freedom.

In the near term, try to just focus on the next step in your relationship, not ten steps ahead, but remember that you have a choice. You can choose to buck the trend of cohabitation and maintain separate places if that is what you and your partner both want.

THE RELATIONSHIPS ARE WORK MYTH

I love love, but I hate the saying "relationships are work." If you're with the right person, they really aren't work at all. Relationships are a mirror, and not a skinny department store kind of mirror. They are an accurate, time-tested mirror that will give you a true-to-life reflection of what you need to work on and where you truly shine. Relationships have the power to transform you into the best or worst version of yourself. Feeling like you're working too hard to keep a relationship together or to get on the same page as your partner is usually a sign of misalignment.

Relationships require effort, clarity, and vulnerability. For some people, that is too big of a burden to bear, but when you find the right relationship, it's like the difference between a job and a career. The work in a relationship is not like the punching-a-clock kind of work; it's the kind of work that you want to show up early for, put in hours on the weekends, and build your future.

Feeling like relationships are work means there's likely a myth waiting to be rewritten or a pillar that just doesn't line up for you. Perhaps you two lack alignment in your goals or you have a mismatch in values. Many times, communication is off or your conflict resolution skills are incompatible. But if you don't have trust, you're fighting an uphill battle. Trust is the last of the Four Pillars to be built, but the one that is most difficult to repair if it has been broken. Trust is the foundation of the healthiest relationships.

THE ELEMENT OF SURPRISE

Even in the most functional relationships, things can get dull. You have to continually re-create that heightened emotional state that you had at the beginning. I do this by putting things to anticipate together on the calendar. When we have a trip on our calendar, even if it's months away, I allow myself to daydream and plan as a way to conjure the same kind of anticipation that we had in the early phase of our relationship.

My husband creates that emotional state through the element of surprise. I promised I would tell you why I remembered the last moment of our first date. It's because he caught me by surprise with an unexpected kiss (consensual, of course). Still today, he surprises me, whether it's a thoughtful and unexpected birthday gift or tickets to a show he knows I'll love. The element of surprise keeps me in curiosity because we have ultimate trust and I know that I'm always safe with him.

For you, it might be surprise, anticipation, or something else entirely, but you can keep coming back to that excitement you felt in the beginning if you and your partner commit to creating it. On *The Drew Barrymore Show*, I was coaching a couple who hoped to reignite the spark in their relationship now that they were new empty-nesters. Before the show, I encouraged them to go back through old photos to reignite memories of those exciting moments they shared when they were younger and first fell in love. We asked each of them to pick a photo on their own and surprise their partner with the picture in the studio. The surprise was on us, though, when they revealed that they both had chosen the same photo of the same happy moment together. By returning to that memory, they accessed those same feelings, and choosing the same moment proved that they were better than soulmates. They had built a strong table together.

HOW DO YOU FIND TRUST?

Trust is a mercurial emotion. It's hard to earn and equally hard to maintain. At its core, trust is about feeling safe. If you feel safe with someone, you can trust that no matter what happens, you will be alright. We tested this in many ways during *A Question of Love*: through having the couples ask and honestly answer deepest, meaningful questions about their past, present, and future; through emotional sessions where I poked and prodded them to find their truth and express it to their partner; and through exercises.

I guided the couples to try partner yoga, to create vision boards together, and even to try a blindfolded trust walk around the neighborhood (just doing it around the house is tough enough). In the end, the couples found that when they let their guard down and were willing to be vulnerable, they could see if they really felt safe with their partner. Testing the relationship in small ways prepares you for the bigger obstacles that are inevitably going to unfold. But you have to move toward the pursuit of your truth. Our brains love stories and they prefer to have clean conclusions over nebulous resolutions. Your mind will drive you to complete the love story as it's still being written, but courage in love means allowing it to unfold truthfully without pushing toward the ending we want.

It's called "falling in love" because you have to be willing to fall. You have to take a leap and know that on the other side of that courageous action, something more beautiful awaits. Most species have a courtship ritual that requires a display of great bravery to win a mate but none quite so dramatic as the bald eagle.

When a potential mate is chosen, they lock talons high in the sky then together they plummet, cartwheeling wildly beak over wing before breaking apart moments before they hit the ground. In humans, love is a similar leap of faith. It takes a moment of courage followed by a moment of surrender and vulnerability to fall in love.

EXERCISE: TWO LETTERS

In addition to some of the exercises I mention above from *A Question of Love*, I also have my clients test out their trust and vulnerability by writing two letters that they never intend to send.

The first letter is directed toward your young self. Begin this exercise looking at a photograph of yourself as a child or visualize your younger self. When you have a picture of your child self in mind, speak from the perspective of your current self addressing a younger self who has no idea what awaits them. Here are some possible prompts for your letter:

1. What did you learn about relationships before that is not true for you today?
2. Is there anything you wish to apologize or make amends for?
3. Are there any promises you wish to make?

In this first letter, you can be completely honest with yourself and you can frame prior hurts or mistakes in a way that allows you to move forward with self-compassion, regardless of what has held you back before.

The second letter is a letter to your partner that says everything you wish you could tell them face-to-face. You can use the questions below to structure it:

1. What do I fear most in this relationship?
2. What do I want most in this relationship?

3. What am I ready to release to make my relationship dream a reality?

4. What do I need from you to feel safe in this relationship?

This exercise, especially when completed after the first letter, can illuminate where you are letting prior conditioning run your relationship future. Understanding your fears and desires will drive you into action. Once the ideas are out on the page with the utmost vulnerability, you can decide what to do with them. Do you want to schedule a time to talk to your partner about what you discovered? Do you want to share the letter with your partner? Do you want to toss away the paper but hold onto the learning and let it guide your next steps in the relationship?

It's easy to get swept up in emotion at the beginning, but in relationships, we are playing the long game, or at least we hope to be. Take your time and develop a curious mind in those first few weeks and months. You're not in a relationship race. It's not a push to clear the next hurdle and cross the finish line to partnership. It's an invitation to integrate everything you've learned so far and see how that shifts the outcome—and you.

So much is revealed in the final phase of dating, and if you're potentially choosing your forever person, rather than letting momentum drive, you should have clarity and conviction in your choice. They say in business you should hire slow and fire fast. So, take your time with relationship onboarding. Your next partnership could be the most important one you have.

THE FUTURE ACTION STEPS

1. *Tune your internal compass.* Understanding your internal cues helps in all areas of your life but especially in dating. The more you listen to your intuition, the more you can trust it to guide your journey.

2. *Quiet your anxiety.* Be mindful and stay in the present to keep anxiety from being in the driver's seat of your life.

3. *Share without expectation.* Opening to another person is one of the bravest things you can do. When you share, others tend to want to share with you too!

4. *Practice slow love.* Love is a long-distance run, not a sprint. Savor the various phases of falling in love and take time to build a strong foundation for your relationship future.

where do we go from here?

THE TRAINER WHO CERTIFIED ME AS A DATING COACH explained why people pay a premium for matchmakers: "They're buying *hopium*," he said. When you hire a matchmaker, you are paying for them to take the burden of finding matches off your plate. You order up what you'd like and their job is to go on the hunt to find your ideal match. Most clients believe that the only problem is that they haven't met the right person and they just need help expanding their dating circle. They hope that a matchmaker knows their soulmate already. If they could just pay someone money to fix this one problem, they'd be in love.

Serial online daters (read: most daters today) are also hooked on hopium. The eternal swipe leads us to believe that our soulmate is hidden out there somewhere beyond these idiots and scam artists. We get our hit of neurochemicals every time we open the dating app, but when we don't see an immediate result, the adrenaline rush that made our heart beat faster and our fingers feel tingly turns into withdrawal. Symptoms of adrenaline withdrawal are depression, anxiety, frustration, and fatigue. If you've dated on an app, this might sound familiar.

People often get to a point of overload, then push away the app entirely and swear off dating. In fact, many daters have written into my show to say they are taking a dating hiatus. When you really consider what that means, it's a completely modern predicament that's actually quite concerning.

Taking a dating hiatus means you are removing yourself from human connection and shutting yourself off from natural impulses. People take hiatuses or abstain from things that are addictive and detrimental to their lives. It's an admission that we are addicted to hopium and that we have to find a more natural balance to keep the emotional and adrenal pendulum from swinging too far in one direction or the other.

What is the cure for our hopium addiction? It's a combination of strategy and self-study. By now, hopefully, you've gleaned that a path of curiosity about yourself can lead to that truth-driven love that Plato mused about. The methods in this book are designed to help you expand your dating pool by first expanding your mind.

You should be curious why your relationships always end after three months or why every ex reminds you in a weird way of your father. You should want to know why you self-sabotage every time it feels a little too good to be true or why your first dates always feel uncomfortable. You can use your dating life and relationships as tools to seek out your truth.

I recognize this is a lofty goal when many people just want a quick hit. They don't want to sort through that massive haystack. They want their soulmate served up to them. Yet, if you haven't examined your relationship patterns and made a conscious decision to relate to partners differently, you're likely to be overcome by a foreboding sense of déjà vu as you move through your dates and into relationships.

You have just completed relationship rehab and now have a simple, reliable system to get off the hopium and onto a healthier way of relating to yourself and your partners.

RELATIONSHIP ROLE MODELS

To dismantle the myths that often overshadow dating discovery, it helps to have a tangible understanding of real-world relationships. Identify at least one relationship role model for yourself. This is a couple you know who seems to have the kind of relationship you imagine for yourself. Ask them if you can interview them or casually talk about their experiences in a relationship so you can develop a well-rounded perception of what it will look and feel like when you are in that dream relationship yourself. Ask questions that illuminate the happy times as well as the challenges. Here are some examples:

- When did you know your spouse was your person?
- How do you handle conflict when it arises?
- What are your favorite memories together?
- What is the toughest thing about being in a relationship?

- What is the most fulfilling thing about being in a relationship?
- Is there anything you misunderstood about your partner that got clearer over time?
- What relationship goals or life goals do you have for the future?

You may find that your path differs from your relationship role models', but having a vision of what a healthy relationship looks like gives you inspiration, even if theirs is different from what you experienced in the past or witnessed in your family growing up. You can also use your relationship role models as your accountability partners to keep you on track with your dating decisions when the going gets tough. They can be a neutral second opinion when you have a confusing situation with a date. They can even be a part of your Connector's Circle and could help you expand your dating pool. To attract love, first you should surround yourself with love—of all types.

THE ODDS

Instead of approaching dating as a quest for one ideal person, what if you thought of finding your person not as a game of Go Fish but rather as a game of poker? Rather than going back to the well every time in search of your matching card, you could win at the game of love with a variety of combinations. Depending on the cards you're dealt, the options are expansive.

Just like playing poker, however, at a certain point in the game, you need to commit to the best hand you think you can build. If you just don't have the cards to pull off a full house but you've told yourself that is the hand you should have, you might end up with nothing. If you take stock of where you are and see an opportunity to make a different play that keeps you in the game, you have to be flexible enough to pivot. Every hand is not going to be a winning hand, and that's why you play the game. But you also can't go into every hand dreaming of getting a royal flush. After all, the mathematical odds of getting a royal flush are 1 in 2,598,960 hands, which is actually far better than 1 in 8 billion, but even so, those aren't great odds to shoot for.

Your odds of finding a satisfying lifelong relationship, however, are actually pretty good. Globally, more than 50 percent of people are married by the age of forty, and even though marriage rates are declining, unmarried cohabitation is becoming more common. Even if it feels like you'll never meet your person, statistically speaking you probably will, though it might take a little longer than it took your parents or grandparents and your partnership may look different from theirs.

Speaking of odds, if you've been to Vegas, you know some people won't sit down at a table because they think the game is rigged and the house always wins. Yet a professional poker player will tell you that it's more skill than luck that gets them the win. Similarly, I meet daters who believe that the dating game is rigged. My inbox is flooded with emails from people who think that if they haven't found love by forty or if they are dating as a single parent or if they just haven't had any luck yet, it must mean that they're doomed in love or that they've somehow been shadow banned in the dating app algorithm (for the record, that's not a thing). They believe that no matter how hard they try, they won't meet their person.

I have helped people in all of these situations and more find love, but your success in dating begins with you. To excel in dating (and in poker), you need to have a combination of skill and faith that you might actually win. If you adopt the mindset that there are many ways to win, you can hit the relationship jackpot.

RECAP

The Mindset, The Search, The Date, The Future—lather, wash, rinse, repeat, this is the life cycle of love. Sometimes we get stuck in one of these phases and we end up repeating it until we either master that skillset or find someone who illuminates where we are stuck, someone whose love makes us want to be the best version of ourselves.

Many times, people hold onto someone because they made it through the first three steps only to find that their relationship can't sustain into the future. I don't see that as a failed attempt. I see each relationship you experience as an opportunity to know yourself better and to find a deeper level of love. Rather than feeling discouraged that you have to start the cycle again, can you flip your perspective and see it as an opportunity to take everything you've learned and do it again with more knowledge and self-awareness?

You are not the same person you were when you began reading this book. You are not the same person you were in your last relationship. You are not locked into a particular future because of your past relationships, your family, or your prior pain. Your mind is changeable, and therefore your actions are changeable, and therefore your experiences are changeable, too. You have the power to rewrite the myths you've accepted over the years.

First, release the List Myth. Rewriting this myth requires you to go against the grain of current dating culture. Apps tell you to list who you are and what you want. Instead, visualize your relationship goals and focus on what's most important in a match. That's a better compass for dating.

Next, abandon the Rules Myth. It's a privilege to write your own rules in dating today. When we are challenged by modern dating, we romanticize the past as a simpler time, but that couldn't be further from the truth. Even if it can feel overwhelming at times, the expansion of our dating options is ultimately more helpful than it is detrimental. Being guided by values helps you stay out of overwhelm and connect with not just anyone in this expanded dating pool but the right people.

Then you can do away with the Chemistry Myth. If you are led by your goals and values, you won't be fooled by chemistry. A deeper feeling of connection will be undeniable when you are communicating with someone with whom you are truly aligned.

Finally, you can retire the Soulmate Myth. Instead, trust your decisions and move forward with confidence that, though you might not have found The One, you have found Your One.

Humans are dynamic and ever-evolving beings, and though it's not easy to find true partnership and connection in our fast-paced world, people are doing it every day. Be mindful of the inputs you're taking in about relationships and how you let your feelings about other people's relationships land. Seeing what is possible for a healthy relationship should inspire you to know that it's possible for you too. Surrounding yourself with a supportive community of others who are positive about love or who are in loving relationships is vitally important. The words you tell yourself about your ability to be loved are powerful, and you are in control of the stories you repeat and the patterns you root yourself in. Your person is somewhere out there right now and there's only one thing left to do. Leave the modern love myths behind and step into the reality of the relationship future that is waiting for you.

That little love cynic in me never set out to rewrite her own love story, but she did realize that the old narratives didn't really fit for her. My story wasn't written all at once. It was crafted day by day and choice by choice. When people used to ask me my five- or ten-year plan, I had trouble answering the question because so much life and so many micro-decisions would happen between now and then. I never fixate on what I want to do in five years; I just ask myself what I want to do *next*. Each next leads to the next next, and through those small moments, I've built my life into something that little girl never imagined was possible.

This plan for love that I've laid out for you might seem like fiction right now, but that's only because you have yet to start writing it. Instead of focusing on the fairy-tale ending, just begin with creating your next chapter. And if you follow the steps I've explained for you here, the story will begin to unfold before your eyes.

On our wedding day, my husband and I had my aunt read an excerpt from Shel Silverstein's poem "The Missing Piece" because it captured exactly how our journey felt until we met one another. In the poem, a circle is looking for its missing piece to fill in its pie-slice-sized gap.

The Pac-Man-like circle rolls around getting into adventures, trying to make pieces fit that are too small or too big or simply not right. Eventually, it finds a piece that looks right, but the circle is so weary from its journey that it can't even believe this piece could work. First, it asks if the piece is anybody else's missing piece. The piece replies, "Not that I know of." Then the circle says, "Well, maybe you want to be your own piece?" To which the piece replies, "I can be someone's and still be my own." That is what it feels like to have found my missing piece and to be married to this person I visualized so long ago.

We have built a steady table with our Four Pillars. We have common goals for the future that evolve as our lives change. We have shared values and live by a similar set of principles. We've resolved conflicts and learned how to communicate clearly with one another. And most importantly, we have trust and mutual respect that we've built in small moments and during honest conversations.

At one point, I didn't believe there was a missing piece for me, yet now I know that I can belong to myself and someone else at the same time. Now that I've been through this journey, it's my greatest joy to help others realize that their missing piece is out there too. Even though you may have had many false starts and uncomfortable pairings, there's another piece out there that's just hoping you'll be a fit for them as well. Whatever your narrative has been up to this point, remember that you always have the power to rewrite your story. The myths had their moment, but great love stories are not written, they're rewritten, and your protagonist deserves a happily ever after.

acknowledgments

Writing a book takes a village. It also takes a swift kick in the pants to get started, a supportive family to give you time and space to get it done, plus a team of mentors, collaborators, advocates, and friends to guide you along the way.

To the pants-kickers: Carol Allen, Lauren Frances, Rachel True, John Kim, Orna Walters, Buy a Vowel Mastermind, and The Homie Hookup, thank you for your guidance and encouragement. This book would still be living inside my mind without you.

To the collaborators: Lindsey Kay Floyd, Scottmarie Nevil, Marquis Olison, Natasha Lewin, Leo Schell, Jimi Vaughn, Ray Christian, and Lauren Passell, thank you for helping me keep the creativity flowing, giving feedback on early drafts, and helping me build the foundation for everything I create.

To the advocates: Leigh Bardugo, Jon Birger, Griff Witte, Logan Ury, and Scout Sobel, you put your reputation on the line and helped set me on this path and I'm forever grateful. My work at the *Washington Post* and the *LA Times* inspired so much of this book and groomed me to become a better writer. Much gratitude to Annys Shin, Alexa McMahon, Lisa Bonos, Rich Juzwiak, and Rene Lynch for your guidance.

To Kyle Gipson, Emily Taber, Christina Palaia, Katie Carruthers-Busser, and everyone at Seal Press and Hachette, thank you for believing in me and shepherding me along the way. Also, thanks to my book coach, Hilary Swanson, for helping me put my passion on the page.

I feel so supported by everyone at New Leaf Literary Agency but especially Jo Volpe and Stephanie Kim, who saw my vision right away. On the TV side, I can't believe I'm so lucky to work with my forever colleague and collaborator Robyn Lattaker-Johnson.

There were people, places, and spaces that made this book a reality. Thank you, Maria Maisto and Trevor Gates, for your hospitality, and Mimi and Lee Hoffman, for your retreat on the Hudson and your never-ending support.

I've had so many mentors along the way, but Inessa Freya, Veronica Alweiss, Rebecca Benenati, and Betsy Crouch have truly changed the trajectory of my life. I'm honored to call them mentors as well as friends.

To Drew Barrymore, your love for love and passion for helping people are inspiring to watch and thrilling to work with. I'm filled with so much gratitude that we connected in the wilderness of the pandemic. Jason Kurtz and the entire team of *The Drew Barrymore Show* literally make miracles happen every day and I'm honored to be a part of the magic.

I have the ultimate respect for all of the amazing producers and TV executives who coaxed me in front of the camera: Chris

Coelen and the Kinetic fam, Joe Livecchi and Dean Slotar, Liz Fine, Gena McCarthy, and the FYI TV folks.

This book wouldn't have been possible without the OkCupid team. Thank you, Melissa Hobley (now at Tinder), Jane Reynolds, and especially Michael Kaye, for your collaboration, your data, and your enthusiasm for helping people find love.

Also thank you to the special folks at the Match Group who I've collaborated with over the years: Amy Canaday, Lauren DeFord, Andrea Lira, and Krystle Ignacio.

Amanda Perez, I am humbled by your salads and your support. Holly Frank, you'll always be my Gayle. Holly Stephens, and we're still together. Scott Sobol, you make NYC feel like home.

Aunt Cess Resnick, I don't know how you see what is possible for me before I can see it myself, but thank you for sending me my first official client and setting me on this path. Cousin Todd, thank you for allowing me to hack your love life. Cousin Ray, thank you for all the moments on the mountaintop. And love to my sisters Dionne and Lanette.

My parents, Lewis Resnick and Jeanette Resnick, filled me with curiosity and made sure that I knew being different was my superpower. You taught me that, with unconditional love, anything is possible, and for that, I'm eternally grateful.

My children, Addie and Julian, teach me the biggest lessons in life and fill my heart with joy, laughter, and creativity. I can't wait to see the love stories and life stories you write for yourselves.

Last but certainly not least, to my husband, Seth Hoffman, my fuzzy life came into focus when I met you. Not only do you have the purest heart and the kindest soul, but you also see the goodness in me and inspire me to be the best version of myself every day. I can say F the Fairy Tale because being married to you is even better than fiction.

To all my listeners, followers, clients, guests, and supporters, thank you for trusting me with your heart. Your happily ever after awaits and I look forward to seeing your new love story unfold.

references

Please note the OkCupid data team pulled dating data for me to use in this book from the company's overall user base. Raw data and analysis are in the author's possession.

Introduction

Ansari, Aziz, and Eric Klinenberg. *Modern Romance*. New York: Penguin Press, 2016.

Galton, Francis. *Hereditary Genius*. London: Macmillan, 1869.

Goodfriend, Wind. *Essentials of Social Psychology*. Audible Originals, 2022.

Julian, Kate. "Why Are Young People Having So Little Sex?" *The Atlantic*, November 13, 2018. https://www.theatlantic.com/magazine/archive/2018/12/the-sex-recession/573949/.

Mather, Mark, Linda A. Jacobsen, Beth Jarosz, Lillian Kilduff, Amanda Lee, Kelvin M. Pollard, Paola Scommegna, and Alicia Vanorman. "America's Changing Population: What to Expect in the 2020 Census." *Population Bulletin* 74, no. 1 (June 2019). https://www.prb.org/wp-content/uploads/2019/06/PRB-PopBulletin-2020-Census.pdf.

Skowronski, Jeanine. "All About the Equal Credit Opportunity Act." Human Rights Campaign, April 14, 2017. https://www.hrc.org/news/all-about-the-equal-credit-opportunity-act.

Stepler, Renee. "Led by Baby Boomers, Divorce Rates Climb for America's 50+ Population." Pew Research Center, March 9, 2017. https://www.pewresearch.org/fact-tank/2017/03/09/led-by-baby-boomers-divorce-rates-climb-for-americas-50-population/.

Steverman, Ben. "Millennials Are Causing the U.S. Divorce Rate to Plummet." Bloomberg, September 25, 2018. https://www.bloomberg.com /news/articles/2018-09-25/millennials-are-causing-the-u-s-divorce-rate -to-plummet.

Thomas S. Eisenstadt, Sheriff of Suffolk County, Massachusetts, Appellant, v. William R. Baird, 405 US 438 (1972). https://www.law.cornell.edu /supremecourt/text/405/438.

US Census Bureau. "Census Bureau Releases New Estimates on America's Families and Living Arrangements." Census.gov, November 29, 2021. https://www.census.gov/newsroom/press-releases/2021/families-and -living-arrangements.html.

———. "Historical Marital Status Tables." Census.gov, November 2022. https://www.census.gov/data/tables/time-series/demo/families/marital.html.

———. "Unmarried and Single Americans Week: September 18–24, 2022." Census.gov, September 18, 2022. https://www.census.gov/newsroom /stories/unmarried-single-americans-week.html.

Wolfinger, Nicholas H. "Contours of the Sex Recession." Institute for Family Studies, March 31, 2021. https://ifstudies.org/blog/contours-of-the-sex -recession.

Part I: The Mindset

Birger, Jon. *Date-onomics: How Dating Became a Lopsided Numbers Game*. New York: Workman Publishing, 2015.

Fisher, Helen E. *Anatomy of Love: A Natural History of Mating, Marriage, and Why We Stray*. New York: W. W. Norton, 2017.

Kondo, Marie. *Life-Changing Magic: Spark Joy Every Day*. New York: Random House, 2015.

Part II: The Search

Barker, Tess. "It Costs $60,000 a Year to Upkeep This Instagram Landmark." Los Angeleno, March 7, 2019. https://losangeleno.com/places /paul-smith-instagram-landmark/.

Blumberg, Perri Ormont. "How Married 'Bachelor' Couples Make It Work. Yes, Some Are Still Together." *New York Times*, March 30, 2022. https:// www.nytimes.com/2022/03/30/style/married-bachelor-couples.html.

Fein, Ellen, and Sherrie Schneider. *The Rules: Time-Tested Secrets for Capturing the Heart of Mr. Right*. New York: Grand Central Publishing, 1995.

OkCupid. "OkCupid's Dating Data Center." Medium, May 2, 2022. https://theblog.okcupid.com/okcupids-dating-data-center-b94589c3c8f3.

Ortiz-Ospina, Esteban. "Who Do We Spend Time with Across Our Lifetime?" Our World in Data, December 11, 2020. https://ourworldindata.org/time-with-others-lifetime.

Potter, Daniel. "Texting Etiquette: A Brief Guide to Polite Messaging." Grammarly, September 28, 2020. https://www.grammarly.com/blog/texting-etiquette/.

Reis, Harry T., Michael R. Maniaci, Peter A. Caprariello, Paul W. Eastwick, and Eli J. Finkel. "Familiarity Does Indeed Promote Attraction in Live Interaction." *Journal of Personality and Social Psychology* 101, no. 3 (2011). https://doi.org/10.1037/a0022885.

Rosenfeld, Michael J., Reuben J. Thomas, and Sonia Hausen. "Disintermediating Your Friends: How Online Dating in the United States Displaces Other Ways of Meeting." *Proceedings of the National Academy of Sciences* 116, no. 36 (2019): 201908630. https://doi.org/10.1073/pnas.1908630116.

Rudder, Christian. *Dataclysm: Love, Sex, Race, and Identity—What Our Online Lives Tell Us About Our Offline Selves*. London: 4th Estate, 2016.

Strauss, Neil. *The Game: Penetrating the Secret Society of Pickup Artists*. New York: Canongate, 2005.

———. *Rules of the Game*. Melbourne: Text Publishing, 2011.

———. *The Truth: An Uncomfortable Book About Relationships*. New York: Dey Street, 2018.

Wang, Wendy. "Marriages Between Democrats and Republicans Are Extremely Rare." Institute for Family Studies, November 3, 2020. https://ifstudies.org/blog/marriages-between-democrats-and-republicans-are-extremely-rare.

Wiseman, Richard. *The Little Book of Luck*. London: Arrow, 2004.

Part III: The Date

Fletcher, Emma. "Reports of Romance Scams Hit Record Highs in 2021." Federal Trade Commission, February 8, 2022. https://www.ftc.gov/news-events/data-visualizations/data-spotlight/2022/02/reports-romance-scams-hit-record-highs-2021.

Gottman, John Mordechai. *Principia Amoris: The New Science of Love*. New York: Routledge, 2014.

Huang, K., M. Yeomans, A. W. Brooks, J. Minson, and F. Gino. "It Doesn't Hurt to Ask." *Journal of Personality and Social Psychology* 113, no. 3 (September 2017): 430–452.

Perez, Sarah. "FTC: US Consumers Lost $770 Million in Social Media Scams in 2021, up 18x from 2017." TechCrunch, January 27, 2022. https:// techcrunch.com/2022/01/27/ftc-u-s-consumers-lost-770-million-in -social-media-scams-in-2021-up-18x-from-2017/.

Prochazkova, Eliska, Luisa Prochazkova, Michael Rojek Giffin, H. Steven Scholte, Carsten K. W. De Dreu, and Mariska E. Kret. "Pupil Mimicry Promotes Trust Through the Theory-of-Mind Network." *Proceedings of the National Academy of Sciences* 115, no. 31 (2018): E7265–E7274. https://doi .org/10.1073/pnas.1803916115.

Ury, Logan. *How to Not Die Alone: The Surprising Science That Will Help You Find Love.* New York: Simon & Schuster, 2021.

Webb, Amy. *Data, a Love Story: How I Gamed Online Dating to Meet My Match.* New York: Penguin, 2014.

Part IV: The Future

"Beating the Odds in Poker—Articles." Bicycle Playing Cards, n.d.

Chapman, Gary D., and Amy Summers. *The Five Love Languages: How to Express Heartfelt Commitment to Your Mate.* Nashville, TN: Lifeway Press, 2010.

Levine, Amir, and Rachel S. F. Heller. *Attached: The New Science of Adult Attachment and How It Can Help You Find—and Keep—Love.* New York: TarcherPerigee, 2012.

Paul, Annie Murphy. *Extended Mind: The Power of Thinking Outside the Brain.* New York: Houghton Mifflin Harcourt, 2021.

Plato. *Plato.* Translated by Benjamin Jowett. London: Arctururs, 2020.

Price, Cynthia J., and Carole Hooven. "Interoceptive Awareness Skills for Emotion Regulation: Theory and Approach of Mindful Awareness in Body-Oriented Therapy (MABT)." *Frontiers in Psychology* 9, no. 798 (2018). https://doi.org/10.3389/fpsyg.2018.00798.

Schwartz, Barry. *The Paradox of Choice: Why More Is Less.* New York: Ecco, 2016.

Suler, John. "The Online Disinhibition Effect." *CyberPsychology & Behavior* 7, no. 3 (2004): 321–326. https://doi.org/10.1089/1094931041291295.

Taylor, Bill. "What Breaking the 4-Minute Mile Taught Us About the Limits of Conventional Thinking." *Harvard Business Review*, March 9, 2018. https://hbr.org/2018/03/what-breaking-the-4-minute-mile-taught-us -about-the-limits-of-conventional-thinking.

index

Damona Hoffman is a celebrity dating coach, host of the award-winning podcast *Dates & Mates*, and the official love expert of *The Drew Barrymore Show*. She has written dating columns for the *LA Times* and the *Washington Post* and hosted episodes of NPR's *Life Kit* podcast. Damona has been a dating expert and spokesperson for many top dating apps, including OkCupid, Match, and Jdate. She lives in Los Angeles with her husband and two children.

DamonaHoffman.com